In The
Yule-Log Glow

Book I

Various Authors

THREE VOLUMES IN ONE.

CHRISTMAS TALES FROM
'ROUND THE WORLD

"Sic as folk tell ower at a winter ingle"
Scott

Editor: **Harrison S. Morris**

[ZHINGOORA BOOKS]

This edition is published by
Zhingoora Books.

The Cover is Designed by Pallav Sethiya.

THE THRESHOLD.

If, gentle reader, you will step across this threshold, now, as the moon rises in the keen Christmas air, and will find a place by the ruddy ingle within-doors, you may hear, if you will, a Babel of voices from many lands, telling over the adventures of the road and falling into the good-fellowship of the happy Christmas season.

Here from the north, with his ample furs thrown back, sits the Russian in friendly talk with a gay little wanderer from Sicilian valleys. There, with elbow crooked by a foaming tankard, leans the German, narrating his perils and pleasures to a gallant Frenchman and a sunbrowned Spaniard who smoke and chatter together as now and then Mynheer stops for a pull at his pipe.

A Swede, Norwegians, an Englishman or two, and even a happy-go-lucky American, are clustered about the Yule-log; for the place you have entered is the common-room of the wide world.

As you slip the latch and take your seat, some traveller calls out: A Merry Christmas! Another cries: A story, a story! and so they fall to, each from his own scrip taking forth a native tale,—and so they sit the midnight out listening and talking in turn; while the good cheer goes round in endless abundance and laughter and song make interludes for the varied narratives.

CONTENTS OF BOOK I.

By Harrison S. Morris.

A Still Christmas[B]

By Agnes Repplier.

Thrond

From the Norwegian of Björnson.

Christmas in the Desert

By Matilda Betham Edwards.

[A] By courtesy of Messrs. W. S. Gottsberger & Co.

[B] By courtesy of "The Catholic World."

A Tale Spoken by a Graybeard Out of the East.

"Gracious powers! Perhaps you are a hundred years old, now I think of it! You look more than a hundred. Yes, you may be a thousand years old for what I know."

Thackeray.

THE THREE KINGS OF COLOGNE.

A CHRISTMAS TALE FROM AN OLD ENGLISH CHRONICLE.

(Written by John of Hildesheim in the Fourteenth Century.)

Here followeth the manner and form of seeking and offering; and also of the burying and translations of the three Holy and Worshipful Kings of Cologne: Jaspar, Melchior, and Balthazar.

Now when the Children of Israel were gone out of Egypt and had won and made subject to them Jerusalem and all the land lying about, so that no man durst set against them in all that country for dread that they had of them; then was there a little hill called Vaws, which was also called the Hill of Victory, and on this hill the ward of them of Ind was ordained and kept by divers sentinels by night and by day against the Children of Israel, and afterward against the Romans; so that if any people at any time purposed with strong hand to enter into the country of the Kingdom of Ind, anon, sentinels of other hills about, through tokens, warned the keepers on the hill of Vaws. And by night they made a great fire and by day they made a great smoke, for that hill Vaws passeth the height of all other hills in all the East. Wherefore, when any such token was seen, then all manner of men made ready to defend themselves from the enemy that approached.

Now in the time when Balaam prophesied of the Star that should betoken the coming of Christ, all the great lords and all the other people of Ind and in the East desired greatly to see the Star of which he spake, and gave gifts to the keepers of the hill of Vaws, and moreover hired them with great rewards, that, if it so were, they saw by day or by night, far or near, any light or any star in the air other than was seen beforetime, anon they should show and send them word. And thus was it that for so long a time the fame of this Star was borne through all the lands of the East; until, of the name of the hill of Vaws, arose up a worshipful and a great kindred in Ind, which is called the progeny of Vaws even unto this day; and there is not a more mighty kindred in all the kingdoms of the East; for this worshipful kindred came first from the King's blood that was named Melchior, that offered gold to our Lord, as ye shall hereafter learn.

In the year of our Lord 1200, when the city of Acon, that in this country is called Akers, flourished and stood in virtue, joy, and prosperity, and was inhabited richly with worshipful princes, and lords, and divers orders of men of religion, and all manner of men of all nations and tongues, so that there was no city like unto it in nobility and might; then, because of its great name and of the marvels that were there, the greatest of birth that were of the progeny of Vaws came out of Ind unto Acon; and when they saw there all things more wonderful than in Ind; then, because of delight, they abode there and made a fair and strong castle for any king or lord. And they brought with them out of the East many rich and wonderful ornaments and jewels. And among all other jewels, they brought a diadem of gold arrayed with precious stones and pearls, and about its edge stood letters of Chaldaic, and a star made like after the Star that appeared to the Three Kings of the East when they sought God, with a sign of the cross, beside.

And that diadem was Melchior's, the king of Nubia and of Araby, that offered gold to the Babe in the manger. And afterward the master of the Order of Templars received this same diadem of gold and many other precious jewels; but when that Order was destroyed the diadem and precious ornaments were lost, and have never been found unto this day. Wherefore there was great sorrow made in all the country for a long time after.

But these same princes of Vaws brought with them out of Ind books written in Hebrew and Chaldaic, concerning the life and deeds of these three blessed Kings, which books were afterward translated into the French tongue: and so, from these books, and from hearsay, and sight, and also from sermons and homilies out of divers other works, the story here written hath been brought together into one book.

And you shall understand that the old kindred of Vaws beareth always in its banner, unto this day, a star with a sign of the cross, made after the same manner as it appeared to the three blessed Kings.

Now it so happened that after Balaam had prophesied of this Star, the more it was sought for the more its fame increased through the land of Ind and Chaldee, and all the people desired to see it.

So they ordained twelve of the wisest and greatest clerks of astronomy that were in all that country about, and gave them great hire to keep watch upon this hill of Vaws for the Star that was prophesied of Balaam. And the cause that there were ordained twelve men was, that if one man died another should be put in his stead; and also that some should keep watch at one time and some another—nevertheless the people looked not only after the Star, but after the Man who was betokened by the Star, the which Man should be Lord of all folk.

And they of Ind and Chaldee who came often into Jerusalem because of merchandise and also for disport—the which, for the most part, be learned in astronomy—said that in Ind were many stars in the firmament that might not be seen by night in Jerusalem; but, specially on this hill of Vaws in clear weather, were seen many and divers strange stars that at the foot of the hill were not seen. Yet this hill of Vaws hath no more breadth than a little chapel is made upon, the which the three worshipful kings did build of stone and timber. And there be about this hill many steps upon which men go up to the chapel on high, and also there grew many good trees and herbs and divers spices all about the hill— for else men might not well go upon this hill because it is so high and so narrow. There is also a pillar of stone made above this chapel, of wondrous height, and in the head of the pillar standeth a great star, well made of gilt, and which turneth with the wind as a vane: and through the light of the sun by day, and of the moon by night, this star gives light a great way about the country. And many other marvels are spoken of this hill of Vaws, the which were long to tell.

Now when the time of grace was come, that God would have mercy on all mankind, in which time the Father of Heaven sent down his Son to take flesh and blood and to be born a man for salvation of all the world: in that time Octavianus, that was Emperor of Rome, sent out a commandment that all the people within his empire should be counted and taxed; and every man went forth from his dwelling-place into his native country. Then came Joseph up from Nazareth unto Bethlehem the city of David, because he was of the household and race of King David, and with him came Mary that was his wife, and also great with child.

And you shall understand that Bethlehem was never of much reputation, neither a place of great quantity. It hath a good site and good ground, for there be many caves and dens under the earth thereabout; and it is distant from Jerusalem but two little miles; and it is but a castle, but is called a city because King David was born there. And in that town was sometime a house which belonged to Isai, the father of David, where David was born and anointed into the kingdom of Israel by Samuel the prophet. And in this same dwelling was the Son of Heaven born of Mary.

And this same house was at the end of a street that was in that time called the Covered Street, because, to keep out the great heat and burning of the sun, this street was canopied above with black cloths and other things,—for such is the use in that country always. And here was wont to be great bargaining, or a fair once a week of old clothes; and specially of trees or timber, by the little house which stood before a den under the earth, made and shaped like a little cellar, where Isai and others that dwelt there after him put certain necessaries that belonged to the household, against the heat of the sun. It is also the manner in all that country that there be certain houses, the which be called the *alchan*, that we call hostelries, and in these houses be mules, horses, asses, and camels always ready, that, if so that any merchant or any man that travelled by the way, be it far or near, need any beast for himself, or for his merchandise, then he goeth to such a house and there he may hire a horse, or what beast that he will, for a certain price. And when he hath such a beast then he goeth from that city to another, where to abide and rest him for a time. Then he dischargeth his beast of his burden, and so sendeth him to a house called there also *alchan*; and the master of the house giveth his beast meat, and, when he may, he sendeth it home to the same place that it came from.

And such a house was, before the birth of Christ, in the place where Christ was born; but, about the time of the Nativity, that house was all destroyed, insomuch that there was nothing left but broken walls on every side, and a little cave under earth, and a little unthrifty house before the cave: and there men sold bread on the same ground; for it is the usage in all that country that all the bread that is sold shall be brought unto a certain place.

Now when Octavianus had sent out a commandment as it is aforesaid, then went Joseph and Mary riding on an ass, late in the eventide, toward the city of Bethlehem, and because they came so late, and all places were occupied with pilgrims and other men, and also because they came in poor array and went about the city, none would receive them, and specially, men say, because that Mary, a young woman, sitting upon an ass, heavy and sorry, and full weary of the way, was near to the time of bearing of her child. Then Joseph led his wife into this shed that none took keep of, down into the little dark house, and there our Lord, Jesus Christ, the same night was born of the Virgin, without any disease or sorrow of her body, for salvation of all mankind.

And in that house, before the cave of old time, was left a manger of the length of a fathom, made in the wall; and to that same manger was an ox of a poor man tied, that none might harbor. And beside that ox Joseph tied his ass, and in that same manger Mary wrapped her blessed Son in cloths and laid Him on high before the ass and the ox,—for there was none other place.

And shepherds were fast by in the same country keeping their sheep in the night, and an angel of Heaven came and stood beside them with a great light, wherefore they were in much dread. And the angel said to them, "Be not afraid, for I tell you a great joy that shall be to all people, for this day is born to us our Lord, Christ, in the city of David, and this shall be to you a token: Ye shall find a young child wrapped in cloths and put in a manger." And then suddenly there came a great multitude of angels of Heaven praising God, who said: "Joy be to God on high and peace in earth to men of good will."

Now the place where the angel appeared to the shepherds that night when Christ was born is but half a mile from Bethlehem, and in that same place David, when he was a child, fed sheep and kept them from the bear and the lion.

Some books say that the shepherds in that country, twice in the year, are wont to keep their sheep in the night, and, therein, times be when the day and the night are both of one length. And you shall understand that the land about Bethlehem is all mountainous for the most part, so that in some places a man shall not well know winter from summer, and in some places it is right cold, and some it is both winter and summer at one time, and sometimes on the mountains, in parts of the East, men shall find snow in the month of August, and that snow is gathered by them that dwell about, and put in caves, and afterward it is borne to the market, where the great lords of the country will buy it, and take it to their houses, and set it in a basin upon their board to make their drink cold.

In September and October, when the sun cometh a little low in that country, then seeds and all manner of herbs commonly begin to wax in the fields, as in this country herbs begin to grow in March and April; also in some parts of the East they reap corn in April and in March, but most in May, as in some places the ground is higher, in some places lower; but beside Bethlehem are many more places of good pasture and of flat ground than elsewhere: insomuch that at Christmas-tide barley beginneth to ear and to wax ripe; and then men send thither, from divers countries, their horses and mules, to make them fat: and that time we call among us Christmas, they call, in their language, the time of herbage. And forasmuch as when Christ was born, peace was in all the world, and betwixt Bethlehem and that place where the angel appeared to the shepherds was but half a mile and a little way more, and also there was no great cold thereabout, therefore the shepherds, all that winter night and day, now in one place, now in another, dwelled there with their sheep, and so they do yet to this day.

Now when Christ was born of the Virgin Mary for salvation of all mankind, then His Star, that was prophesied of Balaam and long awaited and looked for by the twelve astronomers on the hill of Vaws, at that same night and at that same hour, began to arise in the manner of a sun, bright shining; and so after, in the form of an eagle, it ascended above the hill of Vaws. And all that day in highest air it abode without moving, insomuch that when the sun was most hot and most high there was no difference in shining betwixt them.

But when the day of the Nativity was passed, the Star ascended up into the firmament, and it was nothing like to stars that be painted in divers places, for it had right many long streaks and beams, more burning and lighter than a brand of fire; and, as an eagle flying and beating the air with his wings, right so the streaks and beams of the Star stirred it about. And it had in itself the form and likeness of a young child, and above him a sign of the holy cross, and a voice was heard in the Star, saying: "This day is born to us the King of Jews that folk have awaited, and Lord is of them. Go and seek Him and do Him worship!"

Then all the people, both man and woman, of all the country about, when they saw this wonderful and marvellous Star and also heard the voice out of the Star, were greatly aghast and had wonder thereof; but yet they knew well that it was the Star that was prophesied by Balaam, and long time was desired of all the people in that country.

Now when the three worshipful Kings who in that time reigned in Ind, Chaldee, and Persia were informed, by the astronomers, of this Star, they were right glad that they had grace to see the Star in their days. Wherefore these three worshipful Kings, though each of them was far from the other, and none knew of the other's purpose, yet in the same hour the Star appeared to all three, and then they ordained and purposed them, with great and rich gifts and many rich and diverse ornaments that belong to a king's array, and also with mules and camels and horses charged with treasure, and with a great multitude of people, to go seek and worship the Lord and King of the Jews that was new born, as the voice of the Star had commanded. And furthermore they arrayed themselves the much more honestly and worshipfully, because they knew well that he was a worthier King than any of them was.

And you shall understand that there be three Indias, of which these three lords were kings; and all the lands for the most part are islands, and there are also there great waters and wildernesses full of wild and perilous beasts and horrible serpents, and there grow also reeds so high and so great that men make thereof houses and ships. And these isles are divided every one by itself far from the others, so that only with great travail shall a man pass from one kingdom to another.

Now, in the first Ind was the land of Nubia, and therein reigned King Melchior, in the time that Christ was born. Therein also is the land of Araby, in which is the hill Sinai: and a man may lightly sail by the Red Sea out of Egypt and Syria into Ind. In this land is found gold wonderfully red, like thin and small roots, and that gold is the best that is in the world. Herein is also a hill called Bena, where is found a precious stone, called smaragd.

In the second Ind was the kingdom of Godolia, of which Balthazar was king when Christ was born; and this Balthazar offered incense to the Babe; for in this land many more good spices grow than in all the countries of the East, and especially incense, more than in all places of the world; and it droppeth down out of certain trees in the manner of gum.

In the third Ind was the kingdom of Thaars. Of that kingdom was Jaspar king at the birth of Christ. And Jaspar offered myrrh to the young Child, and in this land is the isle of Egrisoulla, where groweth myrrh more plentifully than in any place of the world, and it waxeth like ears of corn that are burnt with the weather, and right thick; and when it is ripe it is so soft that it cleaveth to men's clothes as they go by the way.

Now when these three worshipful Kings were passed forth out of their kingdoms, the Star evenly went before each King and his people, and when they stood still and rested the Star stood still, and when they went forward again the Star always went before them in virtue and strength, and gave light all the way. And, as it is written before, in the time that Christ was born there was peace in all the world, wherefore in all the cities and towns which they went through there was no gate shut neither by night nor by day; and all men of the cities and towns that these worthy Kings went through in the night were wonderfully aghast and passingly marvelled thereof, for they saw kings and vast multitudes go by in great haste; but they knew not what they were, nor whence they came, nor whither they should go. On the morrow the way was greatly befouled with horses' hoofs, whereof they were in much doubt what it might mean, and great altercation was among them for a long time.

Furthermore, these Kings rode forth over hills, waters, valleys, plains, and other divers and perilous places without hindrance or disease, for all the way seemed to them plain and even, and they never took shelter by night nor by day; nor ever rested; nor did their horses or other beasts ever eat or drink till they had come to Bethlehem; and all this time seemed to them but a day.

And thus, through the mercy of God and the leading of the Star, they came unto Jerusalem and Bethlehem the thirteenth day after Christ was born, at the uprising of the sun, whereof is no doubt: for they found Mary and her son in the same place where the Child was born, and laid in the manger.

But when the three blessed Kings, with their host and company were almost come to Jerusalem, saving but two miles, then a great and dark cloud held all the earth, and in that dark cloud they lost the Star. And Melchior with his people was come fast by Jerusalem beside the hill of Calvary, where Christ was afterward crucified; and there the King abode in a cloud of fog and in darkness.

At that time the hill of Calvary was a rock of twelve degrees high, where thieves and other men for divers trespasses were put to death; and there was beside this hill a place where three highways met together. But because of the darkness of the cloud, and also because they knew not the way, they abode there, and went no further at that time.

And next came Balthazar, and he abode under the same cloud, beside the Mount of Olives in a little town that is called Galilee.

Then, when the two Kings were come to these places, the cloud began to ascend and wax clear, yet the Star appeared not. But when they saw that they were near to the city of Jerusalem, knowing not each other, they took their way thither with all their folk; and when they came where the three ways met, then also appeared King Jaspar with all his host. And so these three glorious Kings, each with his host and burdens and beasts, met together in the highway beside the Hill of Calvary. And, notwithstanding that none of them ever before had seen the other, nor knew him, nor had heard of his coming, yet, at their meeting, each one with reverence and joy kissed the other. And they were of diverse language, yet all, seeming, used the same tongue.

So, afterward, when they had spoken together and each had told his purpose and the cause of his journey, and the cause of all was learned to be the same, then they were much more glad and more fervent. And so they rode forth, and suddenly, at the uprising of the sun, they came into the city of Jerusalem. And when they knew that this was the city which the Chaldeans of old time had besieged and destroyed, they were right glad, expecting to have found the King born in that city. But Herod and all his people were greatly disturbed at their sudden coming, for their company and beasts of burden were of so great a number that the city might not receive them, but for the most part they lay without the gates all about, whereof Isaias prophesied: "The strength of folk cometh to thee—that is to say, to the City of Jerusalem—great plenty of camels shall do thee service, and dromedaries of Madyan and Effa shall come to thee. All men shall come from Saba, bringing gold and incense and showing praise to God."

So, these three worshipful Kings, when they were come into the city, asked of the people concerning the Child that was born; and, when Herod heard this, he was troubled and all Jerusalem with him, and he gathered together all his princes and priests and asked them where Christ should be born, and they said: "In Bethlehem of Judea." Then Herod privily summoned to him these three Kings, and learned of them the time that the Star appeared, and so sent them forth unto Bethlehem, saying: "Go and inquire busily of this Child, and when you have found Him, come and tell me, that I may go and do Him worship."

Now when these three Kings were informed of the birth of Christ and of the place where He was born, and so were passed out of Jerusalem, then the Star appeared to them again as it did erst, and went before them till they came to Bethlehem. And fast by that place were the shepherds to whom the angel appeared with great light, showing them the birth of Christ. And the three Kings spake with them, and when the shepherds saw the Star they run together and told how the angel had appeared to them, and furthermore all that the angel had spoken to them. And the Kings were wondrous glad, and with good cheer heard and took consideration of the shepherds' words; and so from witness, and from the words of the shepherds and from the voice of the angel that was heard out of the Star, they had no doubt of the thing. Then anon, when they knew that they were come to Bethlehem, they got down from their horses and changed all their array, and clothed themselves in the best and richest that they had, as kings should be clothed—and always the Star went forth before them.

Now the nearer the Kings came to the place where Christ was born the brighter shined the Star, and they entered Bethlehem the sixth hour of the day. And then they rode through the covered street till they came before that little house. And there the Star stood still, and then descended and shone with so great a light that the little house and the cave within were full of radiance, till anon the Star again went upward into the air, and stood still always above the same place, yet the light ever remained in the house where Christ and Mary were. So as it is said in the Gospel: "They went into the house and found the Child, and fell down and worshipped Him, and offered to Him gifts of gold, myrrh, and incense."

Of this example came afterward a usage, that in all the countries of the East no man should go into the presence of the Sultan, but he brought gold or silver or somewhat else in his hands; and, also, ere he spoke to the Sultan he should kiss the ground, and this is a custom which is used in all the countries of the East to this day. But the Franciscan friars, when they approached the Sultan, offered to him only pears or apples, for they might not touch gold nor silver; and these offerings were received by the Sultan with all reverence and meekness.

Now on the day that the three Kings sought Christ and worshipped Him, He was a little child of thirteen days old, and He was somewhat fat, and lay wrapped in poor clothes in the hay of the manger up to His arms. And Mary, His Mother, as it is written in divers books, was, in person, fleshy and somewhat brown. In the presence of the three Kings she was covered with a poor white mantle, which she held close before her with her left hand. Her head was concealed altogether, save her face, with a linen cloth; and she sat upon the manger and with her right hand held up the young Child's head. And the Kings worshipped Him and kissed His hand devoutly and laid their gifts beside His head.

But what was done with these gifts, ye shall learn hereafter.

Now Melchior, that offered gold to the Holy Child, was the least in stature and person of the three Kings. Balthazar, that offered incense, was of a medium stature; and Jaspar, that offered myrrh, was most in person; whereof is no doubt, for the prophet saith: "Before Him shall fall down Ethiops, and His enemies shall lick the earth. They shall come to Thee that betrayed Thee, and they shall worship the steps of Thy feet." And having regard to the stature of men of that time these Kings were right little of person, insomuch that all manner of people marvelled at them. And this showed well that they were come from far out of the East, for the nearer toward the uprising of the sun that men be born, the less they be of stature and be feebler and more tender.

And you shall understand that these three Kings brought out of their lands many gifts and rich ornaments which King Alexander left in Ind, in Chaldee, and in Persia; and all the ornaments which Queen Saba found in Solomon's temple, and divers vessels that were of the king's house and the Temple of God in Jerusalem, which, in the time of its destruction, were borne into their countries by the Persians and Chaldeans, and many other jewels, both gold and silver, and precious stones, brought they with them to offer to Christ. But when they found our Lord laid on high in the manger and in poor cloths, and the Star that gave so great light in all the place, that it seemed as though they stood in a furnace of fire, then these Kings were so sore afraid that, of all the rich jewels and ornaments they brought with them, they chose nothing, when their treasury was opened, but what came first to their hands, for Melchior took a round apple of gold, as much as a man might hold in his hand, and thirty gilt pennies, and these he offered to our Lord. Balthazar took out of his treasury incense; and Jaspar took out myrrh, as it came first, and that he offered, with weeping and tears.

And the Kings were so aghast and so devout and fervent in their oblations, that to all the words that Mary said they gave but little consideration, save only that to every King as he offered his gifts she bowed down her head meekly, and said, "*Deo gracias*:" that is to say, "I thank God."

When these three Kings had thus performed their way and will, and done all things that they came for, then, as mankind asketh and would, they and all their men and beasts began to eat, and drink, and sleep, and betook them to rest and sport all that day in Bethlehem. For, as is said before, they had neither eaten nor drunk during thirteen days. And then they meekly told to all men in that city how wonderfully the Star had brought them thither from the furthest part of the world.

Now, as the Evangelist saith: A command came to these Kings in their sleep that they should not return again to Herod, and so, by another way, they went home to their kingdoms. But the Star that went before them, appeared no more. And so these three Kings, that suddenly met together at the Mount of Calvary, rode home together with great joy and honor, and rested by the way as men should do.

And they rode through the provinces that Holofernes of old time had traversed with all his hosts, and the people supposed that Holofernes had come again, for as they journeyed into any town they were meekly and worshipfully received, and evermore they told what they had seen, done, and heard, so that their name and praise were never after forgot. But the way that before had taken only thirteen days, through leading of the Star, they found now to take two years, which was ordained, that all men should know what difference is between God's working and man's.

Now, when Herod and the scribes heard that the Kings were gone home again, and came not to him as he had bade them, then, of much envy and malice, he pursued them a great way; and always he found the people bless them, andpraise them, and tell of their nobility. Wherefore Herod burnt and destroyed all the land that was under his power where the Kings had ridden, and especially Tharsis and Cilicia, for he charged them that they had suffered the three Kings privily to pass across the sea in their ships. And Herod's envy was great when he heard how marvellously the Kings had come out of their lands in thirteen days through leading of the Star, and how, afterward, they went home again, without the Star, through guides and interpreters,—yet no man could tell, for wonder, how night and day they passed by; and for this reason the paynims, who had no knowledge of Holy Writ, nor of the birth of Christ, called these three Kings Magos; that is to say, Wise Men of the East.

Now, when the Kings were come with great travail to the Hill of Vaws, they made there, as is aforesaid, a fair chapel in worship of the Child they had sought. Also they made a covenant to meet together at the same place once in the year; and there they ordained their burial. Then all the princes and lords and worshipful knights of their kingdoms, hearing of the return of these three Kings, anon rode forth to them with great, solemnity and met them at the place aforesaid, and with meekness and humility received them. And when they heard how wonderfully God had wrought for their Kings, they held them in more reverence, love, and dread forever after.

So, when the Kings had done what they would, they took leave of each other, and each one, with his people, rode home to his own land with great joy.

And when they were come into their own realms, they preached to all the people what they had seen and done on their journey; and they made in their temples a star after the likeness of that which appeared to them, wherefore many paynims left their errors and worshipped the Holy Child.

And thus these three worshipful Kings dwelt in their kingdoms in honest and devout conversation until the coming of St. Thomas, the apostle.

Now, after the three Kings had gone forth from Bethlehem, there began to wax, all about, a great fame for Mary and her Child, and for the Kings of the East. Wherefore, Mary, in dread of persecution, fled out of the little house where Christ was born, and went to another dark cave and there abode; and divers men and women loved her and ministered to her all manner of necessaries. But when she went out of the little house, Mary forgot and left behind her her smock and the clothes in which Christ was wrapped, folded together and laid in the manger; and there they were, whole and fresh, in the same place to the time when St. Helen, the mother of Emperor Constantine, came thither, long after.

Anon so great was grown Mary's fame that she durst not abide longer there for dread of Herod and the Jews, and an angel appeared to Joseph, saying: "Arise, and take the Child and His mother and flee into Egypt, and tarry there till I summon thee, for it is to come that Herod shall seek the Child to slay Him." Then Joseph arose and took the Child and His mother and went into Egypt in the night, and there he remained until Herod died. And Mary and her Son dwelt in Egypt seven years.

And it is told that by the road which Mary journeyed thither and came back again, grew roses, which are called the Roses of Jericho, and they grow in no other place. The shepherds of that country, in following their sheep, gather these roses in their season, and sell them to pilgrims, and thus they be borne into divers lands. And the place where Mary dwelt is now a garden where groweth balm, and to every bush a Christian man, among the Sultan's prisoners, is assigned to protect it and keep it clean; for when a paynim keepeth them, anon the bushes wax dry and grow no more. And this balm hath many virtues the which were long to tell; but all men in the East believe truly that the place bears such a virtue of growing balm because Mary dwelt there seven years, and washed and bathed her Son in its wells of water.

And as to the gifts which the three Kings gave to Christ: the thirty gilt pennies of Melchior were made of old by Thara, father of Abraham, and Abraham bare them with him when he went on pilgrimage out of the land of Chaldee into Ebron, which was then called Arabia, and there he bought with them a burial-place for himself, his wife, and his children, Isaac and Jacob. In exchange for the same thirty pieces Joseph was sold by his brethren to merchants of Egypt. Afterward, when Jacob died, they were sent to the land of Sheba to buy divers spices and ornaments for his sepulture, and so they were put into the king's treasury of that land. Then by process of time, in Solomon's reign, the Queen of Sheba offered these thirty gilt pennies, with many rich jewels, in the Temple at Jerusalem; but in the time of Roboam, King Solomon's son, when Jerusalem was destroyed and the Temple despoiled, they were carried to the King of Arabia, and were put into his treasury with other spoils from the Temple.

And Melchior offered these same thirty pieces to Christ, because they were of the finest gold, and the best that he had. But when Mary went into Egypt she lost all the gifts of the three Kings by the way, bound all in one cloth together. And it happened there was a shepherd who had so great an infirmity that no leech might heal him, and all that he had he paid to the leeches to be whole,—yet it might not be. But, on a time, as he went into the fields with his sheep, he found these thirty gilt pennies, with incense and myrrh, bound all in a cloth together, and he kept them privily to himself, until, hearing tell of a holy prophet that healed all men of their infirmities by a word, he came to Christ and prayed Him for grace and help; and, being healed, he offered the gold, and incense, and myrrh to Him with good devotion. And when Christ saw the thirty gilt pennies and precious herbs He knew them well, and bade the shepherd go into the Temple and offer them upon the altar.

Now, when the priest saw such oblations laid upon the altar he marvelled much, and took all three things and put them in the common treasury. And afterward, when Judas Iscariot came into the Temple to make covenant with the Princes of the Law to betray his master, they gave him for his pay the same thirty pieces of gold, and for them Judas sold his Master. And after Christ was crucified, then Judas repented, and went to the Temple and cast down to the Princes of the Law the thirty pieces. And with fifteen of these gilt pennies the Jews bought a field of burial for pilgrims; and the other fifteen they gave to the knights who kept the sepulchre of Christ.

And the reason these thirty gilt pennies were called silver in the Gospel, notwithstanding they were fine gold, is, that it is the common usage in that country so to call them, as men in this country call gold from beyond the sea scutys, motouns or florins; moreover in the East the same print is made in gold and silver and copper, and the print on the thirty pieces is this: on one side is a king's head crowned, and on the other are written letters in Chaldaic, which men now cannot read. And many marvels are told of these pieces of gold which were long to tell.

How when Our Lord was ascended into heaven, then he sent St. Thomas, his apostle, into Ind, to preach there God's word. And as St. Thomas went about in the temples he found a star in every one, painted after the manner of the Star that appeared to the three Kings when Christ was born, in which Star was a sign of the Cross and a Child above. And when St. Thomas saw this he asked of the bishops what it was, and they told him that such a Star of old time appeared on the Hill of Vaws in token of a Child that was born who should be king of the Jews, as was heard spoken out of the same Star.

And when St. Thomas had preached and taught the people the understanding of this Star and of the Cross and the Child, then he went to the kingdoms of the three Kings, and he found them whole of body and of a great age. And St. Thomas christened these three Kings and all their people, and the Kings began anon to preach with the Apostle, and when they had converted the people to the law of Christ he ordained them to be Archbishops. And after this St. Thomas was slain, and in all that country where he was martyred both men and women have visages shaped like hounds, yet they be not hairy—and they are so unto this day.

Now under the Hill of Vaws St. Thomas and these three Kings had made a rich city and called it Sewill, and this city is the best and richest city in all the country of Ind to this day; and therein is the habitation of Prester John that is called lord of Ind, and there dwelleth also the Patriarch of Ind who is called Thomas, in worship of St. Thomas and for an everlasting memorial. And when all things were disposed by these three Kings they went to the city of Sewill, and there they lived twelve years.

And a little before the feast of Christ's nativity, when these years were drawn to an end, there appeared a wonderful star above this city and the Kings knew that their time was nigh when they should pass out of this world. Then of one assent they ordained a fair and large tomb for their burial in the church they had made in the city; and in the feast of Christmas they did, solemnly, God's service.

And in the feast of the Circumcision, Melchior, King of Araby, laid him down before all his people and without any disease yielded up his spirit, in the year of his age one hundred and sixteen. Then in the feast of Epiphany, five days thereafter, Balthazar, King of Godolie and Saba, died in the year of his age one hundred and twelve. And then Jaspar the third king, the sixth day after was taken into everlasting joy, and they were all buried in the same tomb that they had ordained; and the Star that appeared over the city before their death, abode always till their bodies were translated unto Cologne, as they of Ind tell.

Now after much time had passed, Queen Helen, the mother of the glorious Emperor Constantine, began to think greatly of the bodies of these three Kings, and she arrayed her with certain people and went into the land of Ind. And she had much praise among the people because of the finding of Mary's smock and the cloths that Christ was wound in in his childhood; and seeing that she was worshipped of all people, the Patriarch Thomas and Prester John, took counsel of other lords and princes and gave her the bodies of King Melchior and King Balthazar. But the Nestorines had borne the body of the third king, King Jaspar, into the isle of Egrisoulla. And these Nestorines were the worst heretics of the world. For the most part they were black Ethiops, who painted Christ and His Mother Mary and the three Kings in their churches all in black, and the Devil all white, in despite of all other Christian men. But because Queen Helen wished not that the three Kings should be parted, she made many prayers and gave great gifts to the chief lords of the isle of Egrisoulla, and thus anon did she get the body of King Jaspar.

And you shall understand that after she had found the bodies of all these three Kings, Queen Helen put them into one chest and arrayed it with great riches, and she brought them unto Constantinople with joy and reverence, and laid them in a church that is called St. Sophia; and this church King Constantine did make—and he alone, with a little child, set up all the pillars of marble.

Now after the death of this worshipful King Constantine and Queen Helen aforesaid, there began a new persecution of heresy against the Christian faith, and of death against them that would maintain the law of Christ. The Greeks forsook the Church and chose a Patriarch for themselves, whom they yet obey until this day.

Now in this persecution the bodies and the relics of the three holy Kings were put at no reverence, but utterly set at naught. For the Saracens and Turks at this time won with strong battle the lands of Greece and Armenia, and destroyed a great part of these lands.

Then came an Emperor of Rome who was called Mauricius, and through the help of them of Milan he recovered all these lands again, and, as is said among men in that country, through counsel of this Emperor the bodies of the three Kings were carried unto Milan, and they were there laid with all solemnity and worship in a fair church which is called after St. Eustorgio, because he had asked the bodies from the Emperor, and being granted them had sent them unto Milan.

Then afterward by process of time, it happed that the city of Milan began to rebel against the Emperor, who was called Frederick I., and this Emperor sent to the Archbishop of Cologne, who was called Rainald, for help. Then this Archbishop, through help of divers lords of the land of Milan, took the city of Milan and destroyed a great part thereof. And the chief men of the city took the bodies of the three Kings and hid them privily in the earth.

Now among all others there was in Milan a lord named Asso, and the Emperor hated him more than all the rest of its people. So it happed that in the destruction of the city the Archbishop won Asso's palace through strong hand, and lived therein a great while, for Asso was taken and put into prison.

Then, anon, Asso sent privily by his keepers to the Archbishop of Cologne and prayed him that he would come and speak with him, and it was granted that Asso should go to the Archbishop. And when he was come to him, he prayed him that, if he would get him grace of the Emperor and his love and the restoration of his lordship, he would give him the bodies of the three Kings.

When the Archbishop heard this, he went to the Emperor and prayed for Lord Asso, and got him grace and love. And when this was done, Asso brought, secretly, the three bodies of the Kings to the Archbishop of Cologne.

Then the Archbishop sent the bodies forth, by private means, a great way out of the city of Milan, whereupon he went to the Emperor anew and prayed him that he would grant him these three bodies, and the Emperor did so with good will. Then the Archbishop openly, with great solemnity and procession, brought the three holy Kings unto Cologne, and there put them in the fair church of St. Peter, worshipfully; and all the people of the country, with all the reverence they might, received these holy relics; and there they are kept and beholden of all manner of nations unto this day.

Thus endeth the translation of these Three Worshipful Kings: Melchior, Balthazar, and Jaspar.

A French Yeoman's Legend.

"He laughed fit to make the plates rattle, his little brown eyes twinkling all the while."

Erckmann-Chatrian.

THE THREE CHRISTMAS MASSES.

I.

"Two truffled turkeys, Garrigou?"

"Yes, reverend Father, two magnificent turkeys stuffed with truffles. There's no mistake, for I helped to stuff them myself. The flesh almost cracked as they roasted, it was so tight—so——"

"Holy Virgin! and I, who love truffles as——Hurry; give me my surplice, Garrigou. And what else besides the turkeys; what else did you see in the kitchen?"

"Oh! all sorts of good things. Since noon we've done nothing but pluck pheasants, pewits, wood-hens, and heath-cocks. Feathers are scattered thick. Then from the pond they've brought eels and golden carp and trout, and——"

"What size are the trout, Garrigou?"

"Oh, as big as that! reverend Father. Enormous!"

"Heavens, I seem to see them! Have you put the wine in the flasks?"

"Yes, reverend Father, I've put the wine in the flasks. But what's a mouthful or two as you go to midnight Mass! You should see the dining-hall in the château, full of decanters that sparkle with wine of every color. And the silver dishes, above all the ornamented ones; the flowers; the candlesticks! I never saw anything to equal it. Monsieur the Marquis has invited all the nobility of the neighborhood. You will be at least forty at table, without counting either the bailiff or the notary. Ah! it will make you very happy to be there, reverend Father. Why, only to smell the delicious turkeys—the odor of truffles pursues me even yet. Muh!"

"Come, come, Garrigou, you must guard against the sin of greediness, and especially on the night of the Nativity. Quickly, now, light the candles and sound the first bell for Mass; midnight is very near, and we must not be late."

This conversation was held on Christmas night, in the year of grace sixteen hundred and sixteen, between the reverend Dom Balaguère, formerly prior of Barnabites, now chaplain in the service of the Sires de Trinquelague, and his clerk Garrigou; or at least what he supposed was his clerk Garrigou, because you will learn that the devil had that night taken on the round face and wavering traits of the young sacristan, the better to tempt the reverend Father to commit the dreadful sin of gluttony. Now, while the supposed Garrigou (hum! hum!) rung, with all his might, the bells of the seignorial chapel, the reverend Father put on his chasuble in the little sacristy of the château; and, his mind already becoming troubled by the gastronomic descriptions he had heard, he repeated to himself:

"Roasted turkeys; golden carp; trout as large as that!"

Outside, the night wind blew, scattering the music of the bells, and one by one lights began to appear in the shadows about the flanks of Mont Ventoux, upon the summit of which rose the ancient towers of Trinquelague. These lights were carried by the farmers on their way to attend midnight Mass at the château. They climbed the paths in groups of five or six, the father leading, lantern in hand, the women enveloped in their big brown mantles, where their infants nestled for shelter. In spite of the hour and the cold all these honest people marched cheerfully on, sustained by the thought that when they came out from the Mass they would find, as they did each year, tables spread for them below in the kitchens. Now and again on the rough ascent, the coach of some seigneur, preceded by torch-bearing porters, reflected in its glasses the cold moonlight; or, maybe, a mule trotted along shaking his bells, and in the light of the lanterns covered with frost, the farmers recognized their bailiff and saluted him as he passed:

"Good-evening, good-evening, Master Arnoton."

"Good-evening, good-evening, my children."

The night was clear, the stars were polished with cold, the wind stung, and a fine sleet, which glistened on the clothes without wetting them, kept faithfully the tradition of Christmases white with snow. Raised there aloft, the château appeared like the goal of all things, with its enormous mass of towers and gables, the belfry of its chapel mounting into the blue-black sky, and a crowd of small lights that winked, went and came, twinkled at all the windows, and seemed, on the sombre background of the building, like sparks running through the cinders of burnt paper. Once past the drawbridge and the postern, it was necessary, in order to gain the chapel, to traverse the first courtyard, full of coaches, of valets, of sedan-chairs, and bright with the flare of torches and the fires of the kitchens. There was the click of the turnspits, the crash of stewpans, the noises of glass and silver preparing for the dinner. From below, a warm vapor, which smelt of roasting meat and the strong herbs of curious sauces, whispered to the farmers, to the chaplain, to the bailiff—to all the world:

"What a revel we are going to have after Mass!"

II.

Drelindin din! Drelindin din! Midnight Mass is about to begin. In the chapel of the château, a miniature cathedral with arches intercrossed and a wainscot of oak mounting as high as the walls, all the hangings have been arranged, all the candles lit.

And what a host of people! And what toilettes! First, seated in the sculptured stall which surrounds the choir, behold the Sire de Trinquelague in a suit of salmon-colored taffeta; and next to him all the invited nobles. Facing these, on a prie-dieu trimmed with velvet, is the old dowager Marquise in her robe of fire-colored brocade, and the young Dame de Trinquelague, surmounted by a huge head-dress of lace, made in the latest fashion of the French court. Further down, dressed in black, with vast pointed perukes and shaven faces, are the bailiff, Thomas Arnoton, and the notary, Master Ambroy, two grave objects among the flowing silks and figured damasks. Then come the fat majordomos, the pages, the grooms, the attendants; dame Barbe, all her keys suspended at her side on a ring of thin silver. At the bottom of the hall, on the benches, are the servants, the yeomen with their families; and lastly, beyond, all about the doors as they open and shut discretely, are the scullions, who steal in, between two sauces, to get a little of the Mass, carrying an odor of the revelry into the church, all in its gay attire and warm with so many burning candles.

Is it a glimpse of their little white caps that distracts the celebrant of the Mass? Or, it may be the clangor made by Garrigou's bells, that pulsating sound which shakes the altar with an infernal vibration and seems to say all the time:

"Hurry up, hurry up. We'll soon be done; we'll soon be at table!"

The fact is, that each time it sounds—that peal of the devil—the chaplain forgets his Mass and thinks of nothing but the coming revel. He pictures to himself the uproar of the kitchens; the furnace heated like a blacksmith's forge; the vapor of opening trenchers, and in that vapor two magnificent turkeys, buttered, tender, bursting with truffles.

Or, perhaps he saw pass the files of little pages bearing dishes enveloped in tempting steam, and, with them, entered the grand saloon already prepared for the feast. O deliciousness! behold the immense table all set and sparkling; the peacocks in their plumes; the pheasants with their open wings of reddish-brown; the ruby-colored flagons; the pyramids of fruit peeping from green branches; and those marvellous fish of which Garrigou told (ah! well, yes, Garrigou!) held aloft on a bed of fennel, the mother-of-pearl scales as bright as when they came from the water, with a bouquet of odorous herbs in their monster-like nostrils. So distinct is the vision of these marvels, that it seems to Dom Balaguère as if all the wonderful dishes are served before him on the embroideries of the altar-cloth; and two or three times, in place of *Dominus vobiscum*, he is surprised to find himself repeating the *Benedicite*. Saving these slight mistakes, the holy man does his office very conscientiously, without skipping a line, without omitting a genuflexion; and all goes well enough as far as the end of the first Mass; because, you know, on Christmas night the same celebrant must repeat three consecutive Masses.

"One!" said the chaplain, with a sigh of relief; then, without losing a minute, he made a sign to his clerk—or the person he believed to be his clerk, and——

Drelindin din! Drelindin din!

The second Mass begins, and with it begins also the sin of Dom Balaguère.

"Hurry, hurry, let's get done," cries the thin voice of Garrigou's bell, and this time the unlucky priest, abandoning himself to the demon of gluttony, rushes through the missal, devouring its pages with all the avidity of an overcharged appetite. Frantically he bows; arises; makes the signs of the cross, goes through the genuflexions, abbreviates all his gestures, the sooner to be finished. Scarcely does he extend his arms to the Gospel, or strike his breast where it is required. Between the clerk and him it is a race which shall jabber the faster. Verse and response hurry each other, tumble over each other. The words, hardly pronounced, because it takes too much time to open the mouth, become incomprehensible murmurs.

Oremus ps—ps—ps—
Meâ culpâ—pâ—pâ—.

Like hard-working vintagers pressing grapes in a vat, both wade through the Latin of the Mass, splashing it on all sides.

"*Dom—scum!*" says Balaguère.

"*Stutuo!*" responds Garrigou, and all the while the damnable chime sounds in their ears, like those little bells put on the post-horses to make them gallop more swiftly. Believe me, under such conditions a low Mass is vastly expedited!

"Two!" said the chaplain, all out of breath; then without taking time to breathe, red, perspiring, he tumbled down the stairs of the altar.

Drelindin din! Drelindin din! The third Mass begins.

Only a step or so and then the dining-hall! but, alas, the nearer the revel approaches, the more the unfortunate Balaguère is seized with the very folly of impatience and greediness. His vision accentuates it; the golden carp, the roast turkeys are there. He may touch them—he may—Oh, Holy Virgin! the dishes steam; the wines send forth sweet odors; and shaking out its reckless song, the bell cries to him:

"Hurry up, hurry up; still faster, still faster!"

But how can he go any faster? He scarcely moves his lips, he pronounces fully not a single word. He tries to cheat the good God altogether of His Mass, and that is what brings his ruin. By temptation upon temptation, he begins to jump one verse, then two. Then the epistle is too long—he does not finish it; skims the Gospel, passes by the creed without even entering, skips the pater, salutes from afar the preface, and by bounds and jumps precipitates himself into eternal damnation, always following the infamous Garrigou (*vade retro, Satanas*), who seconds him with marvellous skill; tucks up his chasuble, turns the leaves two by two, disarranges the music-desk, reverses the flagons, and unceasingly rings the bell more and more vigorously, more and more quickly.

You should have seen what a figure all the assistants cut. Obliged to follow, like mimics, a Mass of which they did not understand a word, some rose when others kneeled, or seated themselves when others stood, and all the actors in this singular office mixed themselves on the benches in numberless contrary attitudes.

The star of Christmas, on its journey through the heavens yonder by the little manger, paled with astonishment at the confusion.

"The Abbe's in a dreadful hurry: I can't follow him at all," said the aged dowager, shaking her head-dress with bewilderment. Master Arnoton, his great steel spectacles on his nose, searched in his prayer-book where the deuce the words could be. But, after all, that gallant host, which itself was thinking only of the feast, was far from being vexed because the Mass rode post; and when Balaguère, with beaming countenance, turned toward the assembly crying with all his might, *Ite missa est*, with a single voice they returned, *Deo gratias*, so joyously, so fervently, that one might have thought them already at table responding to the first toast of the night.

III.

Five minutes later the crowd of seigneurs was seated in the grand dining-hall, the chaplain in the midst of them. The château, illuminated from top to bottom, echoed with songs, cries, laughter, uproar, and the venerable Dom Balaguère planted his fork in the wing of a wood-hen, drowning the remorse of his sin under floods of wine of the Pope and the sweet juices of the meats.

So much did he eat and drink, that the poor holy man died in the night of a terrible attack of sickness, without having even time to repent. Then near the morning he arrived in heaven with all the savor of the feast still about him and I leave you to imagine how he was received:

"Retire from my sight, evil Christian!" said the Sovereign Judge, "thy fault is dark enough to efface a whole life of virtue. Ah, thou hast robbed me of a Mass to-night. Thou shalt pay me back three hundred in its place, and thou shalt not enter into Paradise unless thou shalt have celebrated in thy proper chapel these three hundred Christmas Masses in the presence of all those who have sinned by thy fault and with thee."

This, then, is the true legend of Dom Balaguère as they tell it in the land of olives. To-day the château of Trinquelague is no more, but the chapel still stands erect on the summit of Mont Ventoux, in a grove of green oaks. The wind beats its disjointed portal; the grass creeps across its threshold; the birds have built in the angles of the altar and in the embrasures of the high windows, whence the colored panes have long ago vanished. But it appears that every year at Christmas, a supernatural light runs about these ruins, and that, in going to Mass or feast, the peasants see the chapel illuminated by invisible candles which burn brightly even through the wind and snow.

You may laugh if you will, but a vine-dresser of the neighborhood named Garrigue, without doubt a descendant of Garrigou, has assured me that one Christmas night, finding himself a little so-so-ish, he became lost on the mountain beside Trinquelague, and behold what he saw! At eleven o'clock, nothing. All was silent, dark, lifeless. Suddenly, toward midnight, a chime sounded up above from a clock, an old, old chime which seemed six leagues away. Pretty soon, on the ascending road, Garrigue saw lights trembling in the uncertain shadows. Under the porch of the chapel somebody walked, somebody whispered:

"Good-evening, Master Arnoton."

"Good-evening, good-evening, my children."

When the whole company was entered, my vine-dresser, who was exceedingly brave, approached stealthily, and peeping through the broken door saw a strange spectacle. All those who had passed him were ranged about the choir, in the ruined nave, as if the ancient benches still existed. Beautiful dames in brocade with coifs of lace; seigneurs bedizzened from top to toe; peasants in flowered jackets like those of our grandfathers,—everything with an ancient air, faded, dusty, worn-out. Now and then the night-birds, habitual dwellers in the chapel, awakened by all these lights, winged about the candles, whose flames mounted straight and vague as if they burnt behind gauze. And what amused Garrigue most was a certain personage with great steel spectacles, who shook at each instant his high black peruke, on which one of the birds had alighted and entangled itself, silently beating its wings.

At the farthest end, a little old man of boyish size, on his knees in the midst of the choir, pulled desperately at the chimeless and silent bell; while a priest attired in ancient gold, went and came before the altar reciting orisons of which one heard not a single word. Surely, that was Dom Balaguère in the act of saying his third low Mass.

A Love-Passage from a Wandering Cossack.

"Dressed in his everlasting blue frock, he sat near the fire playing cards."

Turgenieff.

A RUSSIAN CHRISTMAS PARTY.

Count Rostow's affairs were going from bad to worse. He was of a warm, generous nature, with unlimited faith in his servants, and hence was blind to the mismanagement and dishonesty which had sapped his fortune. The possessor of a handsome establishment at the Russian capital, Moscow, the owner of rich provincial estates, and the inheritor of a noble name and wealth, he was nevertheless on the verge of ruin. He had given up his appointment as *Maréchal de la Noblesse*, which he had gone to his seat of Otradnoë to assume, because it entailed too many expenses; and yet there was no improvement in the state of his finances.

Nicolas and Natacha, his son and daughter, often found their father and mother in anxious consultation, talking in low tones of the sale of their Moscow house or of their property in the neighborhood. Having thus retired into private life, the count now gave neither fêtes nor entertainments. Life at Otradnoë was much less gay than in past years; still, the house and domain were as full of servants as ever, and twenty persons or more sat down to dinner daily. These were dependants, friends, and intimates, who were regarded almost as part of the family, or at any rate seemed unable to tear themselves away from it: among them a musician named Dimmler and his wife, Ioghel the dancing-master and his family, and old Mlle. Bélow, former governess of Natacha and Sonia, the count's niece and adopted child, and now the tutor of Pétia, his younger son; besides others who found it simpler to live at the count's expense than at their own. Thus, though there were no more festivities, life was carried on almost as expensively as of old, and neither the master nor the mistress ever imagined any change possible. Nicolas, again, had added to the hunting establishment; there were still fifty horses in the stables, still fifteen drivers; handsome presents were given on all birthdays and fête days, which invariably wound up as of old with a grand dinner to all the neighborhood; the count still played whist or boston, invariably letting his cards be seen by his friends, who were always ready to make up his table, and relieve him without hesitation of the few hundred roubles which constituted their principal income. The old man marched on blindfold through the tangle of his pecuniary difficulties, trying to conceal them, and only succeeding in augmenting them; having neither the courage nor the patience to untie the knots one by one.

The loving heart by his side foresaw their children's ruin, but she could not accuse her husband, who was, alas! too old for amendment; she could only seek some remedy for the disaster. From her woman's point of view there was but one: Nicolas's marriage, namely, with some rich heiress. She clung desperately to this last chance of salvation; but if her son should refuse the wife she should propose to him, every hope of reinstating their fortune would vanish. The young lady whom she had in view was the daughter of people of the highest respectability, whom the Rostows had known from her infancy: Julie Karaguine, who, by the death of her second brother, had suddenly come into great wealth.

The countess herself wrote to Mme. Karaguine to ask her whether she could regard the match with favor, and received a most flattering answer. Indeed, Mme. Karaguine invited Nicolas to her house at Moscow, to give her daughter an opportunity of deciding for herself.

Nicolas had often heard his mother say, with tears in her eyes, that her dearest wish was to see him married. The fulfilment of this wish would sweeten her remaining days, she would say, adding covert hints as to a charming girl who would exactly suit him. One day she took the opportunity of speaking plainly to him of Julie's charms and merits, and urged him to spend a short time in Moscow before Christmas. Nicolas, who had no difficulty in guessing what she was aiming at, persuaded her to be explicit on the matter, and she owned frankly that her hope was to see their sinking fortunes restored by his marriage with her dear Julie!

"Then, mother, if I loved a penniless girl, you would desire me to sacrifice my feelings and my honor—to marry solely for money?"

"Nay, nay; you have misunderstood me," she said, not knowing how to excuse her mercenary hopes. "I wish only for your happiness!" And then, conscious that this was not her sole aim, and that she was not perfectly honest, she burst into tears.

"Do not cry, mamma; you have only to say that you really and truly desire it, and you know I would give my life to see you happy; that I would sacrifice everything, even my feelings."

But this was not his mother's notion. She asked no sacrifice, she would have none; she would sooner have sacrificed herself, if it had been possible.

"Say no more about it; you do not understand," she said, drying away her tears.

"How could she think of such a marriage?" thought Nicolas. "Does she think that because Sonia is poor I do not love her? And yet I should be a thousand times happier with her than with a doll like Julie."

He stayed in the country, and his mother did not revert to the subject. Still, as she saw the growing intimacy between Nicolas and Sonia, she could not help worrying Sonia about every little thing, and speaking to her with colder formality. Sometimes she reproached herself for these continual pin-pricks of annoyance, and was quite vexed with the poor girl for submitting to them with such wonderful humility and sweetness, for taking every opportunity of showing her devoted gratitude, and for loving Nicolas with a faithful and disinterested affection which commanded her admiration.

Just about this time a letter came from Prince André, dated from Rome, whither he had gone to pass the year of probation demanded by his father as a condition to giving consent to his son's marriage with the Countess Natacha. It was the fourth the Prince had written since his departure. He ought long since to have been on his way home, he said, but the heat of the summer had caused the wound he had received at Austerlitz to reopen, and this compelled him to postpone his return till early in January.

Natacha, though she was so much in love that her very passion for Prince André had made her day-dreams happy, had hitherto been open to all the bright influences of her young life; but now, after nearly four months of parting, she fell into a state of extreme melancholy, and gave way to it completely. She bewailed her hard fate, she bewailed the time that was slipping away and lost to her, while her heart ached with the dull craving to love and be loved. Nicolas, too, had nearly spent his leave from his regiment, and the anticipation of his departure added gloom to the saddened household.

Christmas came; but, excepting the pompous high Mass and the other religious ceremonies, the endless string of neighbors and servants with the regular compliments of the season, and the new gowns which made their first appearance on the occasion, nothing more than usual happened on that day, or more extraordinary than twenty degrees of frost, with brilliant sunshine, a still atmosphere, and at night a glorious starry sky.

After dinner, on the third day of Christmas-tide, when every one had settled into his own corner once more, ennui reigned supreme throughout the house. Nicolas, who had been paying a round of visits in the neighborhood, was fast asleep in the drawing-room. The old count had followed his example in his room. Sonia, seated at a table in the sitting-room, was copying a drawing. The countess was playing out a "patience," and Nastacia Ivanovna, the old buffoon, with his peevish face, sitting in a window with two old women, did not say a word.

Natacha came into the room, and, after leaning over Sonia for a minute or two to examine her work, went over to her mother and stood still in front of her.

The countess looked up. "Why are you wandering about like a soul in torment? What do you want?" she said.

"Want! I want him!" replied Natacha, shortly, and her eyes glowed. "Now, here—at once!"

Her mother gazed at her anxiously.

"Do not look at me like that; you will make me cry."

"Sit down here."

"Mamma, I want him, I want him! Why must I die of weariness?" Her voice broke and tears started from her eyes. She hastily quitted the drawing-room and went to the housekeeper's room, where an old servant was scolding one of the girls who had just come in breathless from out-of-doors.

"There is a time for all things," growled the old woman. "You have had time enough for play."

"Oh, leave her in peace, Kondratievna," said Natacha. "Run away, Mavroucha—go."

Pursuing her wandering, Natacha went into the hall; an old man-servant was playing cards with two of the boys. Her entrance stopped their game and they rose. "And what am I to say to these?" thought she.

"Nikita, would you please go—what on earth can I ask for?—go and find me a cock; and you, Micha, a handful of corn."

"A handful of corn?" said Micha, laughing.

"Go, go at once," said the old man.

"And you, Fédor, can you give me a piece of chalk?"

Then she went on to the servants' hall and ordered the samovar to be got ready, though it was not yet tea-time; she wanted to try her power over Foka, the old butler, the most morose and disobliging of all the servants. He could not believe his ears, and asked her if she really meant it. "What next will our young lady want?" muttered Foka, affecting to be very cross.

No one gave so many orders as Natacha, no one sent them on so many errands at once. As soon as a servant came in sight she seemed to invent some want or message; she could not help it. It seemed as though she wanted to try her power over them; to see whether, some fine day, one or another would not rebel against her tyranny; but, on the contrary, they always flew to obey her more readily than any one else.

"And now what shall I do, where can I go?" thought she, as she slowly went along the corridor, where she presently met the buffoon.

"Nastacia Ivanovna," said she, "if I ever have children, what will they be?"

"You! Fleas and grasshoppers, you may depend upon it!"

Natacha went on. "Good God! have mercy, have mercy!" she said to herself. "Wherever I go it is always, always the same. I am so weary; what shall I do?"

Skipping lightly from step to step, she went to the upper story and dropped in on the Ioghels. Two governesses were sitting chatting with M. and Mme. Ioghel; dessert, consisting of dried fruit, was on the table, and they were eagerly discussing the cost of living at Moscow and Odessa. Natacha took a seat for a moment, listened with pensive attention, and then jumped up again. "The island of Madagascar!" she murmured, "Ma-da-gas-car!" and she separated the syllables. Then she left the room without answering Mme. Schoss, who was utterly mystified by her strange exclamation.

She next met Pétia and a companion, both very full of some fireworks which were to be let off that evening. "Pétia!" she exclaimed, "carry me down-stairs!" And she sprang upon his back, throwing her arms round his neck; and, laughing and galloping, they thus scrambled along to the head of the stairs.

"Thank you, that will do. Madagascar!" she repeated; and, jumping down, she ran down the flight.

After thus inspecting her dominions, testing her power, and convincing herself that her subjects were docile, and that there was no novelty to be got out of them, Natacha settled herself in the darkest corner of the music-room with her guitar, striking the bass strings, and trying to make an accompaniment to an air from an opera that she and Prince André had once heard together at St. Petersburg. The uncertain chords which her unpractised fingers sketched out would have struck the least experienced ear as wanting in harmony and musical accuracy, while to her excited imagination they brought a whole train of memories. Leaning against the wall and half hidden by a cabinet, with her eyes fixed on a thread of light that came under the door from the rooms beyond, she listened in ecstasy and dreamed of the past.

Sonia crossed the room with a glass in her hand. Natacha glanced round at her and again fixed her eyes on the streak of light. She had the strange feeling of having once before gone through the same experience—sat in the same place, surrounded by the same details, and watching Sonia pass carrying a tumbler. "Yes, it was exactly the same," she thought.

"Sonia, what is this tune?" she said, playing a few notes.

"What, are you there?" said Sonia, startled. "I do not know," she said, coming closer to listen, "unless it is from 'La Tempête';" but she spoke doubtfully.

"It was exactly so," thought Natacha. "She started as she came forward, smiling so gently; and I thought then, as I think now, that there is something in her which is quite lacking in me. No," she said aloud, "you are quite out; it is the chorus from the 'Porteur d'Eau'—listen," and she hummed the air. "Where are you going?"

"For some fresh water to finish my drawing."

"You are always busy and I never. Where is Nicolas?"

"Asleep, I think."

"Go and wake him, Sonia. Tell him to come and sing."

Sonia went, and Natacha relapsed into dreaming and wondering how it had all happened. Not being able to solve the puzzle, she drifted into reminiscence once more. She could see him—him—and feel his impassioned eyes fixed on her face. "Oh, make haste back! I am so afraid he will not come yet! Besides, it is all very well, but I am growing old; I shall be quite different from what I am now! Who knows? Perhaps he will come to-day! Perhaps he is here already! Here in the drawing-room. Perhaps he came yesterday and I have forgotten."

She rose, laid down the guitar, and went into the next room. All the household party were seated round the tea-table,—the professors, the governesses, the guests; the servants were waiting on one and another—but there was no Prince André.

"Ah, here she is," said her father. "Come and sit down here." But Natacha stopped by her mother without heeding his bidding.

"Oh, mamma, bring him to me, give him to me soon, very soon," she murmured, swallowing down a sob. Then she sat down and listened to the others. "Good God! always the same people! always the same thing! Papa holds his cup as he always does, and blows his tea to cool it as he did yesterday, and as he will to-morrow."

She felt a sort of dull rebellion against them all; she hated them for always being the same.

After tea Sonia, Natacha, and Nicolas huddled together in their favorite, snug corner of the drawing-room; that was where they talked freely to each other.

"Do you ever feel," Natacha asked her brother, "as if there was nothing left to look forward to; as if you had had all your share of happiness, and were not so much weary as utterly dull?"

"Of course I have. Very often I have seen my friends and fellow-officers in the highest spirits and been just as jolly myself, and suddenly have been struck so dull and dismal, have so hated life, that I have wondered whether we were not all to die at once. I remember one day, for instance, when I was with the regiment; the band was playing, and I had such a fit of melancholy that I never even thought of going to the promenade."

"How well I understand that! I recollect once," Natacha went on, "once when I was a little girl, I was punished for having eaten some plums, I think. I had not done it, and you were all dancing, and I was left alone in the school-room. How I cried! cried because I was so sorry for myself, and so vexed with you all for making me so unhappy."

"I remember; and I went to comfort you and did not know how; we were funny children then; I had a toy with bells that jingled, and I made you a present of it."

"Do you remember," said Natacha, "long before that, when we were no bigger than my hand, my uncle called us into his room, where it was quite dark, and suddenly we saw——"

"A negro!" interrupted Nicolas, smiling at her recollection. "To be sure. I can see him now; and to this day I wonder whether it was a dream or a reality, or mere fancy invented afterwards."

"He had white teeth and stared at us with his black eyes."

"Do you remember him, Sonia?"

"Yes, yes—but very dimly."

"But papa and mamma have always declared that no negro ever came to the house. And the eggs; do you remember the eggs we used to roll up at Easter; and one day how two little grinning old women came up through the floor and began to spin round the table?"

"Of course. And how papa used to put on his fur coat and fire off his gun from the balcony. And don t you remember——?" And so they went on recalling, one after the other, not the bitter memories of old age, but the bright pictures of early childhood, which float and fade on a distant horizon of poetic vagueness, midway between reality and dreams. Sonia remembered being frightened once at the sight of Nicolas in his braided jacket, and her nurse promising her that she should some day have a frock trimmed from top to bottom.

"And they told me you had been found in the garden under a cabbage," said Natacha. "I dared not say it was not true, but it puzzled me tremendously."

A door opened, and a woman put in her head, exclaiming, "Mademoiselle, mademoiselle, they have fetched the cock!"

"I do not want it now; send it away again, Polia." said Natacha.

Dimmler, who had meanwhile come into the room, went up to the harp, which stood in a corner, and in taking off the cover made the strings ring discordantly.

"Edward Karlovitch, play my favorite nocturne—Field's," cried the countess, from the adjoining room.

Dimmler struck a chord. "How quiet you young people are," he said, addressing them.

"Yes, we are studying philosophy," said Natacha, and they went on talking of their dreams.

Dimmler had no sooner begun his nocturne than Natacha, crossing the room on tiptoe, seized the wax-light that was burning on the table and carried it into the next room; then she stole back to her seat, it was now quite dark in the larger room, especially in their corner, but the silvery moonbeams came in at the wide windows and lay in broad sheets on the floor.

"Do you know," whispered Natacha, while Dimmler, after playing the nocturne, let his fingers wander over the strings, uncertain what to play next, "when I go on remembering one thing beyond another, I go back so far, so far, that at last I remember things that happened before I was born, and——"

"That is metempsychosis," interrupted Sonia, with a reminiscence of her early lessons. "The Egyptians believed that our souls had once inhabited the bodies of animals, and would return to animals again after our death."

"I do not believe that," said Natacha, still in a low voice, though the music had ceased. "But I am quite sure that we were angels once, somewhere there beyond, or, perhaps, even here; and that is the reason we remember a previous existence."

"May I join the party?" asked Dimmler, coming towards them.

"If we were once angels, how is it that we have fallen lower?"

"Lower? Who says that it is lower? Who knows what I was?" Natacha retorted with full conviction. "Since the soul is immortal, and I am to live forever in the future, I must have existed in the past, so I have eternity behind me, too."

"Yes; but it is very difficult to conceive of that eternity," said Dimmler, whose ironical smile had died away.

"Why?" asked Natacha. "After to-day comes to-morrow, and then the day after, and so on forever; yesterday has been, to-morrow will be——"

"Natacha, now it is your turn; sing me something," said her mother. "What are you doing in that corner like a party of conspirators?"

"I am not at all in the humor, mamma," said she; nevertheless she rose. Nicolas sat down to the piano; and standing, as usual, in the middle of the room, where the voice sounded best, she sang her mother's favorite ballad.

Though she had said she was not in the humor, it was long since Natacha had sung so well as she did that evening, and long before she sang so well again. Her father, who was talking over business with Mitenka in his room, hurriedly gave him some final instructions as soon as he heard the first note, as a schoolboy scrambles through his tasks to get to his play; but as the steward did not go, he sat in silence, listening, while Mitenka, too, standing in his presence, listened with evident satisfaction. Nicolas did not take his eyes off his sister's face, and only breathed when she took breath. Sonia was under the spell of that exquisite voice and thinking of the gulf of difference that lay between her and her friend, full conscious that she could never exercise such fascination. The old countess had paused in her "patience,"—a sad, fond smile played on her lips, her eyes were full of tears, and she shook her head, remembering her own youth, looking forward to her daughter's future and reflecting on her strange prospects of marriage.

Dimmler, sitting by her side, listened with rapture, his eyes half closed.

"She really has a marvellous gift!" he exclaimed. "She has nothing to learn,—such power, such sweetness, such roundness!"

"And how much I fear for her happiness!" replied the countess, who in her mother's heart could feel the flame that must some day be fatal to her child's peace.

Natacha was still singing when Pétia dashed noisily into the room to announce, in triumphant tones, that a party of mummers had come.

"Idiot!" exclaimed Natacha, stopping short, and, dropping into a chair, she began to sob so violently that it was some time before she could recover herself. "It is nothing, mamma, really nothing at all," she declared, trying to smile. "Only Pétia frightened me; nothing more." And her tears flowed afresh.

All the servants had dressed up, some as bears, Turks, tavern-keepers, or fine ladies; others as mongrel monsters. Bringing with them the chill of the night outside, they did not at first venture any farther than the hall; by degrees, however, they took courage; pushing each other forward for self-protection, they all soon came into the music-room. Once there, their shyness thawed; they became expansively merry, and singing, dancing, and sports were soon the order of the day. The countess, after looking at them and identifying them all, went back into the sitting-room, leaving her husband, whose jovial face encouraged them to enjoy themselves.

The young people had all vanished; but half an hour later an old marquise with patches appeared on the scene—none other than Nicolas; Pétia as a Turk; a clown—Dimmler; a hussar—Natacha; and a Circassian—Sonia. Both the girls had blackened their eyebrows and given themselves mustaches with burned cork.

After being received with well-feigned surprise, and recognized more or less quickly, the children, who were very proud of their costumes, unanimously declared that they must go and display them elsewhere. Nicolas, who was dying to take them all for a long drive en troïka,[c] proposed that, as the roads were in splendid order, they should go, a party of ten, to the Little Uncle's.

[C]A team of three horses harnessed abreast.

"You will disturb the old man, and that will be all," said the countess. "Why, he has not even room for you all to get into the house! If you must go out, you had better go to the Mélukows'."

Mme. Mélukow was a widow living in the neighborhood; her house, full of children of all ages, with tutors and governesses, was distant only four versts from Otradnoë.

"A capital idea, my dear," cried the count, enchanted. "I will dress up in costume and go, too. I will wake them up, I warrant you!"

But this did not at all meet his wife's views. Perfect madness! For him to go out with his gouty feet in such cold weather was sheer folly! The count gave way, and Mme. Schoss volunteered to chaperon the girls. Sonia's was by far the most successful disguise; her fierce eyebrows and mustache were wonderfully becoming, her pretty features gained expression, and she wore the dress of a man with unexpected swagger and smartness. Something in her inmost soul told her that this evening would seal her fate.

Sonia

In a few minutes four sleighs with three horses abreast to each, their harness jingling with bells, drew up in a line before the steps, the runners creaking and crunching over the frozen snow. Natacha was the foremost, and the first to tune her spirits to the pitch of this carnival freak. This mirth, in fact, proved highly infectious, and reached its height of tumult and excitement when the party went down the steps and packed themselves into the sleighs, laughing and shouting to each other at the top of their voices. Two of the sleighs were drawn by light cart-horses, to the third the count's carriage horses were harnessed, and one of these was reputed a famous trotter from Orlow's stable; the fourth sleigh, with its rough-coated, black shaft-horse, was Nicolas's private property. In his marquise costume, over which he had thrown his hussar's cloak, fastened with a belt round the waist, he stood gathering up the reins. The moon was shining brightly, reflected in the plating of the harness and in the horses' anxious eyes as they turned their heads in uneasy amazement at the noisy group that clustered under the dark porch. Natacha, Sonia, and Mme. Schoss, with two women servants, got into Nicolas's sleigh; Dimmler and his wife, with Pétia, into the count's; the rest of the mummers packed into the other sleighs.

"Lead the way, Zakhare!" cried Nicolas, to his father's coachman, promising himself the pleasure of outstripping him presently; the count's sleigh swayed and strained, the runners, which the frost had already glued to the ground, creaked, the bells rang out, the horses closed up for a pull, and off they went over the glittering, hard snow, flinging it up right and left like spray of powdered sugar. Nicolas started next, and the others followed along the narrow way, with no less jingling and creaking. While they drove under the wall of the park the shadows of the tall, skeleton trees lay on the road, checkering the broad moonlight; but as soon as they had left it behind them, the wide and spotless plain spread on all sides, its whiteness broken by myriads of flashing sparks and spangles of reflected light. Suddenly a rut caused the foremost sleigh to jolt violently, and then the others in succession; they fell away a little, their intrusive clatter breaking the supreme and solemn silence of the night.

"A hare's tracks!" exclaimed Natacha, and her voice pierced the frozen air like an arrow.

"How light it is, Nicolas," said Sonia. Nicolas turned round to look at the pretty face with its black mustache, under the sable hood, looking at once so far away and so close in the moonshine. "It is not Sonia at all," he said, smiling.

"Why, what is the matter?"

"Nothing," said he, returning to his former position.

When they got out on the high-road, beaten and ploughed by horses' hoofs and polished with the tracks of sleighs, his steeds began to pull and go at a great pace. The near horse, turning away his head, was galloping rather wildly, while the horse in the shafts pricked his ears and still seemed to doubt whether the moment for a dash had come. Zakhare's sleigh, lost in the distance, was no more than a black spot on the white snow, and as he drew farther away the ringing of the bells was fainter and fainter; only the shouts and songs of the maskers rang through the calm, clear night.

"On you go, my beauties!" cried Nicolas, shaking the reins and raising his whip. The sleigh seemed to leap forward, but the sharp air that cut their faces and the flying pace of the two outer horses alone gave them any idea of the speed they were making. Nicolas glanced back at the other two drivers; they were shouting and urging their shaft-horses with cries and cracking of whips, so as not to be quite left behind; Nicolas's middle horse, swinging steadily along under the shaft-bow, kept up his regular pace, quite ready to go twice as fast the moment he should be called upon.

They soon overtook the first troïka, and after going down a slope they came upon a wide cross-road running by the side of a meadow.

"Where are we, I wonder," thought Nicolas; "this must be the field and slope by the river. No—I do not know where we are! This is all new and unfamiliar to me! God only knows where we are! But no matter!" And smacking his whip with a will, he went straight ahead. Zakhare held in his beasts for an instant, and turned his face, all fringed with frost, to look at Nicolas, who came flying onward.

"Steady there, sir!" cried the coachman, and leaning forward, with a click of his tongue he urged his horses in their turn to their utmost speed. For a few minutes the sleighs ran equal, but before long, in spite of all Zakhare could do, Nicolas gained on him and at last flew past him like a lightning flash; a cloud of fine snow, kicked up by the horses, came showering down on the rival sleigh; the women squeaked, and the two teams had a struggle for the precedence, their shadows crossing and mingling on the snow.

Then Nicolas, moderating his speed, looked about him; before, behind, and on each side of him stretched the fairy scene; a plain strewn with stars and flooded with light.

"To the left, Zakhare says. Why to the left?" thought he. "We were going to the Mélukows'. But we are going where fate directs or as Heaven may guide us. It is all very strange and most delightful, is it not?" he said, turning to the others.

"Oh! look at his eyelashes and beard; they are quite white!" exclaimed one of the sweet young men, with pencilled mustache and arched eyebrows.

"That I believe is Natacha?" said Nicolas. "And that little Circassian—who is he? I do not know him, but I like his looks uncommonly! Are you not frozen?" Their answer was a shout of laughter.

Dimmler was talking himself hoarse, and he must be saying very funny things, for the party in his sleigh were in fits of laughing.

"Better and better," said Nicolas to himself; "now we are in an enchanted forest—the black shadows lie across a flooring of diamonds and mix with the sparkling of gems. That might be a fairy palace, out there, built of large blocks of marble and jewelled tiles? Did I not hear the howl of wild beasts in the distance? Supposing it were only Mélukovka that I am coming to after all! On my word, it would be no less miraculous to have reached port after steering so completely at random!"

It was, in fact, Mélukovka, for he could see the house servants coming out on the balcony with lights, and then down to meet them, only too glad of this unexpected diversion.

"Who is there?" a voice asked within.

"The mummers from Count Rostow's; they are his teams," replied the servants.

Pélaguéia Danílovna Mélukow, a stout and commanding personality, in spectacles and a flowing dressing-gown, was sitting in her drawing-room surrounded by her children, whom she was doing her best to amuse by modelling heads in wax and tracing the shadows they cast on the wall, when steps and voices were heard in the ante-room. Hussars, witches, clowns, and bears were rubbing their faces, which were scorched by the cold and covered with rime, or shaking the snow off their clothes. As soon as they had cast off their furs they rushed into the large drawing-room, which was hastily lighted up. Dimmler, the clown, and Nicolas, the marquise, performed a dance, while the others stood close along the wall, the children shouting and jumping about them with glee.

"It is impossible to know who is who—can that really be Natacha? Look at her; does not she remind you of some one? Edward, before Karlovitch, how fine you are! and how beautifully you dance! Oh! and that splendid Circassian—why, it is Sonia! What a kind and delightful surprise; we were so desperately dull. Ha, ha! what a beautiful hussar! A real hussar, or a real monkey of a boy—

which is he, I wonder? I cannot look at you without laughing." They all shouted and laughed and talked at once, at the top of their voices.

Natacha, to whom the Mélukows were devoted, soon vanished with them to their own room, where corks and various articles of men's clothing were brought to them, and clutched by bare arms through a half-open door. Ten minutes later all the young people of the house rejoined the company, equally unrecognizable. Pélaguêïa Danílovna, going and coming among them all, with her spectacles on her nose and a quiet smile, had seats arranged and a supper laid out for the visitors, masters and servants alike. She looked straight in the face of each in turn, recognizing no one of the motley crew—neither the Rostows, nor Dimmler, nor even her own children, nor any of the clothes they figured in.

"That one, who is she?" she asked the governess, stopping a Kazan Tartar, who was, in fact, her own daughter. "One of the Rostows, is it not? And you, gallant hussar, what regiment do you belong to?" she went on, addressing Natacha. "Give some *pastila* to this Turkish lady," she cried to the butler; "it is not forbidden by her religion, I believe."

At the sight of some of the reckless dancing which the mummers performed under the shelter of their disguise, Pélaguêïa Danílovna could not help hiding her face in her handkerchief, while her huge person shook with uncontrollable laughter—the laugh of a kindly matron, frankly jovial and gay.

When they had danced all the national dances, ending with the *Horovody*, she placed every one, both masters and servants, in a large circle, holding a cord with a ring and a rouble, and for a while they played games. An hour after, when the finery was the worse for wear and heat and laughter had removed much of the charcoal, Pélaguéïa Danilovna could recognize them, compliment the girls on the success of their disguise, and thank the whole party for the amusement they had given her. Supper was served for the company in the drawing-room, and for the servants in the large dining-room.

"You should try your fortune in the bathroom over there; that is enough to frighten you!" said an old maid who lived with the Mélukows.

"Why?" said the eldest girl.

"Oh! you would never dare to do it; you must be very brave."

"Well, I will go," said Sonia.

"Tell us what happened to that young girl, you know," said the youngest Mélukow.

"Once a young girl went to the bath, taking with her a cock and two plates with knives and forks, which is what you must do; and she waited. Suddenly she heard horses' bells—some one was coming; he stopped, came up-stairs, and she saw an officer walk into the room; a real live officer—at least so he seemed—who sat down opposite to her where the second cover was laid."

"Oh! how horrible!" exclaimed Natacha, wide-eyed. "And he spoke to her—really spoke?"

"Yes, just as if he had really been a man. He begged and prayed her to listen to him, and all she had to do was to refuse him and hold out till the cock crowed; but she was too much frightened. She covered her face with her hands, and he clasped her in his arms; luckily some girls who were on the watch rushed in when she screamed."

"Why do you terrify them with such nonsense?" said Pélaguéia Danilovna.

"But, mamma, you know you wanted to try your fortune too."

"And if you try your fortune in a barn, what do you do?" asked Sonia.

"That is quite simple. You must go to the barn—now, for instance—and listen. If you hear thrashing, it is for ill-luck; if you hear grain dropping, that is good."

"Tell us, mother, what happened to you in the barn."

"It is so long ago," said the mother, with a smile, "that I have quite forgotten; besides, not one of you is brave enough to try it."

"Yes, I will go," said Sonia. "Let me go."

"Go by all means if you are not afraid."

"May I, Madame Schoss?" said Sonia to the governess.

Now, whether playing games or sitting quietly and chatting, Nicolas had not left Sonia's side the whole evening; he felt as if he had seen her for the first time, and only just now appreciated all her merits. Bright, bewitchingly pretty in her quaint costume, and excited as she very rarely was, she had completely fascinated him.

"What a simpleton I must have been!" thought he, responding in thought to those sparkling eyes and that triumphant smile which had revealed to him a little dimple at the tip of her mustache that he had never observed before.

"I am afraid of nothing," she declared. She rose, asked her way, precisely, to the barn, and every detail as to what she was to expect, waiting there in total silence; then she threw a fur cloak over her shoulders, glanced at Nicolas, and went on.

She went along the corridor and down the back-stairs; while Nicolas, saying that the heat of the room was too much for him, slipped out by the front entrance. It was as cold as ever, and the moon seemed to be shining even more brightly than before. The snow at her feet was strewn with stars, while their sisters overhead twinkled in the deep gloom of the sky, and she soon looked away from them, back to the gleaming earth in its radiant mantle of ermine.

Nicolas hurried across the hall, turned the corner of the house, and went past the side door where Sonia was to come out. Half-way to the barn stacks of wood, in the full moonlight, threw their shadows on the path, and beyond, an alley of lime-trees traced a tangled pattern on the snow with the fine crossed lines of their leafless twigs. The beams of the house and its snow-laden roof looked as if they had been hewn out of a block of opal, with iridescent lights where the facets caught the silvery moonlight. Suddenly a bough fell crashing off a tree in the garden; then all was still again. Sonia's heart beat high with gladness; as if she were drinking in not common air, but some life-giving elixir of eternal youth and joy.

"Straight on, if you please, miss, and on no account look behind you."

"I am not afraid," said Sonia, her little shoes tapping the stone steps and then crunching the carpet of snow as she ran to meet Nicolas, who was within a couple of yards of her. And yet not the Nicolas of every-day life. What had transfigured him so completely? Was it his woman's costume with frizzed-out hair, or was it that radiant smile which he so rarely wore, and which at this moment illumined his face?

"But Sonia is quite unlike herself, and yet she is herself," thought Nicolas on his side, looking down at the sweet little face in the moonlight. He slipped his arms under the fur cloak that wrapped her, and drew her to him, and he kissed her lips, which still tasted of the burned cork that had blackened her mustache.

"Nicolas—Sonia," they whispered; and Sonia put her little hands round his face. Then, hand in hand, they ran to the barn and back, and each went in by the different doors they had come out of.

Natacha, who had noted everything, managed so that she, Mme. Schoss, and Dimmler should return in one sleigh, while the maids went with Nicolas and Sonia in another. Nicolas was in no hurry to get home; he could not help looking at Sonia and trying to find under her disguise the true Sonia—his Sonia, from whom nothing now could ever part him. The magical effects of moonlight, the remembrance of that kiss on her sweet lips, the dizzy flight of the snow-clad ground under the horses' hoofs, the black sky, studded with diamonds, that bent over their heads, the icy air that seemed to give vigor to his lungs—all was enough to make him fancy that they were transported to a land of magic.

"Sonia, are you not cold?"

"No; and you?"

Nicolas pulled up, and giving the reins to a man to drive, he ran back to the sleigh in which Natacha was sitting.

"Listen," he said, in a whisper and in French; "I have made up my mind to tell Sonia."

"And you have spoken to her?" exclaimed Natacha, radiant with joy.

"Oh, Natacha, how queer that mustache makes you look! Are you glad?"

"Glad! I am delighted. I did not say anything, you know, but I have been so vexed with you. She is a jewel, a heart of gold. I—I am often naughty, and I have no right to have all the happiness to myself now. Go, go back to her."

"No. Wait one minute. Mercy, how funny you look!" he repeated, examining her closely and discovering in her face, too, an unwonted tenderness and emotion that struck him deeply. "Natacha, is there not some magic at the bottom of it all, heh?"

"You have acted very wisely. Go."

"If I had ever seen Natacha look as she does at this moment I should have asked her advice and have obeyed her, whatever she had bid me do; and all would have gone well. So you are glad?" he said, aloud. "I have done right?"

"Yes, yes, of course you have! I was quite angry with mamma the other day about you two. Mamma would have it that Sonia was running after you. I will not allow any one to say—no, nor even to think—any evil of her, for she is sweetness and truth itself."

"So much the better." Nicolas jumped down and in a few long strides overtook his own sleigh, where the little Circassian received him with a smile from under the fur hood; and the Circassian was Sonia, and Sonia beyond a doubt would be his beloved little wife!

When they got home the two girls went into the countess's room and gave her an account of their expedition; then they went to bed. Without stopping to wipe off their mustaches they stood chattering as they undressed; they had so much to say of their happiness, their future prospects, the friendship between their husbands:

"But, oh! when will it all be? I am so afraid it will never come to pass," said Natacha, as she went toward a table on which two looking-glasses stood.

"Sit down," said Sonia, "and look in the glass; perhaps you will see something about it." Natacha lighted two pairs of candles and seated herself. "I certainly see a pair of mustaches," she said, laughing.

"You should not laugh," said the maid, very gravely.

Natacha settled herself to gaze without blinking into the mirror; she put on a solemn face and sat in silence for some time, wondering what she should see. Would a coffin rise before her, or would Prince André presently stand revealed against the confused background in the shining glass? Her eyes were weary and could hardly distinguish even the flickering light of the candles. But with the best will in the world she could see nothing; not a spot to suggest the image either of a coffin or of a human form. She rose.

"Why do other people see things and I never see anything at all? Take my place, Sonia; you must look for yourself and for me, too. I am so frightened; if I could but know!"

Sonia sat down and fixed her eyes on the mirror.

"Sofia Alexandrovna will be sure to see something," whispered Douniacha; "but you always are laughing at such things." Sonia heard the remark and Natacha's whispered reply: "Yes, she is sure to see something; she did last year." Three minutes they waited in

76

total silence. "She is sure to see something," Natacha repeated, trembling.

Sonia started back, covered her face with one hand, and cried out:

"Natacha!"

"You saw something? What did you see?" And Natacha rushed forward to hold up the glass.

But Sonia had seen nothing; her eyes were getting dim, and she was on the point of giving it up when Natacha's exclamation had stopped her; she did not want to disappoint them; but there is nothing so tiring as sitting motionless. She did not know why she had called out and hidden her face.

"Did you see him?" asked Natacha.

"Yes; stop a minute. I saw him," said Sonia, not quite sure whether "him" was to mean Nicolas or Prince André. "Why not make them believe that I saw something?" she thought. "A great many people have done so before, and no one can prove the contrary. Yes, I saw him," she repeated.

"How? standing up or lying down?"

"I saw him—at first there was nothing; then suddenly I saw him lying down."

"André, lying down? Then he is ill!" And Natacha gazed horror-stricken at her companion.

"Not at all; he seemed quite cheerful, on the contrary," said she, beginning to believe in her own inventions.

"And then—Sonia, what then?"

"Then I saw only confusion—red and blue."

"And when will he come back, Sonia? When shall I see him again? O God! I am afraid for him—afraid of everything."

And, without listening to Sonia's attempts at comfort, Natacha slipped into bed, and, long after the lights were out, she lay motionless but awake, her eyes fixed on the moonshine that came dimly through the frost-embroidered windows.

A Wayfarer's Fancy.

"A felicitous combination of the German, the Sclave, and the Semite, with grand features, brown hair floating in artistic fashion, and brown eyes in spectacles."

George Eliot.

TWO CHRISTMASES.

I.

It was the time of the great war. Germany was desolated. Towns and villages were destroyed by flames. Order and law had given way to savage power; and from the walls of many a ruined house of God the wooden image of the Saviour looked down with a face of anguish on the horrors of the degenerate times.

The terrified citizens of towns that were still untouched by war, hid themselves within their narrow walls, awaiting, in tremulous fear, the day on which their homes must also fall a prey to plundering soldiers. If any one were obliged to go beyond the boundaries, he would glance anxiously at the bushes on either side of the road; and when night came on, he would be forced to look with horror and sorrow at the reddened horizon, where a little village or lonely hamlet was burning to ashes.

But who is it cowers there in the ditch by the highway? A dried-up little man with deathly-pale countenance, and clad in a black coat! Flee, Wanderer! let him not gaze at you with his piercing gray eyes! Beware! for that old man is the Plague-man!

The heart of the Wanderer sinks within him. Horrified he rushes away, and thanks heaven when, in the gray of the morning, he sees again the towers of his native town. Enraptured by the sight of home he believes these towers with the dear, well-known faces can protect him; but the old cripple has been quicker than he. Before break of day he has knocked at the town-gate, and the gate-keeper, on opening it, has scarcely looked into his gray eyes before he sank down as though some one had felled him with an axe.

Then the gray old man begins his terrible work. Like a bat he slips into all dwellings; no gate and no bolt is an obstacle to him. Right up into the lofts he climbs and opens the most secret chamber. That threshold he passes is doomed to the Black-death.

It had happened thus to a little town in Franconia, where but a few houses remained untouched by the terrible plague. In this town there lived a poor, honest couple with their child, a boy of nearly three years. Their cottage lay on a small hill, and was divided from the road by a little garden. People ascribed it to this that the awful spirit for a long time had left their home untouched. But at last he seemed to have found his way to even this out-of-the-way place.

A few days before Christmas the boy fell sick, and on Christmas morning he lay motionless in bed, so that the poor parents thought the plague had taken their child from them. The father wanted to bury the body at once, but the mother showed him the rosy cheeks of the dead child, and said that a death that looked so like sleep could do them no harm. Thereupon she went into the little garden and cut box-tree leaves from under the snow, and made a wreath for the dead darling. She placed the wreath on his curly head and moved his bed into the middle of the room, where she set candles burning around it, just as we do in quieter times for a dear departed one. Then she went into the wood, cut down a small Christmas-tree and placed it, all decorated with lights, nuts, and bright tinsel, next to the coffin, in order that the dead child might also have his Christmas pleasure.

This was the only Christmas-tree that the poor stricken town lit up! People passing along the road looked with secret jealousy at the illuminated window, wondering how they could still rejoice in such bitter times. But no gladsome sounds from the window reached the street, where flake after flake was whirling down from the gray heavens, covering everything in its white cloak. And unceasingly, as flake after flake sank down to earth, so in the little chamber the tears of the poor woman rolled down her cheeks till the lights of the Christmas-tree burned low, the fire in the stove died away, and sleep closed the streaming eyes of the mother. Then all was quiet, very quiet, in the little chamber.

But at the gates of Heaven it was very noisy that evening. Countless hosts were crowding up the broad stairway, young and old, rich and poor: a mixed and motley crowd. There the patrician elbowed the tailor who had made his coat; the general the lowest sutler; and a ragged beggar was even next to a king, who drew his purple closer around him in order not to be contaminated. All were pushing towards the great, light gate, and many a one, who on earth had only beaten and jostled others, received here in the crowd his own first jostling. At the gate stood a beautiful, tall angel, who sprinkled each one with water out of a golden vessel. The touch of this water obliterated at once all remembrance of the past.

St. Peter, who considered the noise and bustle too much of a good thing, was of the opinion that mankind had none of the bother of dying, all the work falling on him; and he was accordingly grumbling to himself. Suddenly he saw a little fellow, clad only in a shirt, standing before him, shivering all over, and regarding him with innocent, childish eyes, as if asking whether he might enter. St. Peter, unwilling that such little folks should cause delay in business, said, roughly, "In with you!" The little frightened fellow rushed, thereupon, so quickly through the gate that the angel did not have time to sprinkle him with the waters of oblivion.

Now, as children of two years have but short memories and very harmless pasts, the angel smilingly let him slip by. Once inside, little Hans was seized by a host of flying angels and whirled away to Paradise, which was more beautiful than the fairest garden on earth. Rare plants with big, magnificently colored blossoms filled the air with spicy odor. Here dwelt the tiny children who had left earth before they knew anything of it. Here they could dream on forever; and their breath swept softly over every bud. Large butterflies with silken wings were bathing in the clear ether, and floating entranced from bud to bud. The heavens glittered and lightened as though composed of millions of diamonds; yet the sun did not blind the eye, nor the warmth rise to summer heat. Eternal spring had banished from these regions battle and death, tempest and decay, and far away below in misty distance lay all the sorrows of tormented creation. Amongst the flowers wandered blissful forms, absorbed in the beauty of surrounding harmony.

The boy curiously observed all this splendor, peered into the dewy buds of the flowers, examined the wings of his heavenly playmates, and was not a little rejoiced on observing that two wings had also grown on him, with which he could fly like a bird. "If neighbor Liesel could only see me!" thought Hans, and he felt quite proud at the thought. For, notwithstanding all the splendor about him, the picture of his parents' home presented itself constantly to his little mind. He had an excellent memory of the much despised earth, which soon with magnetic power drew all his thoughts towards it. At the sight of the wonderful flowers of Paradise, such as the earth never produces, he could think of nothing but the violets, and crocuses, and tulips which curled up in spring-time out of the black earth of his father's garden. The golden fruits on the trees reminded him of the gilded ones of the Christmas-tree, and seemed to him even brighter; and although the Paradise of heaven, with its eternal clearness, was a thousand times more beautiful than the changing air below, yet the little heart felt a dim yearning for the beloved earth, the griefs of which he had not yet learned to measure; and, amidst all this angelic beauty, he only felt an uncontrollable longing for the plain, human countenance of his mother. Then there came an end to his enjoyment. He began to cry, and, finally, to roar lustily. The other little angels gathered astonished around him, staring at the strange playmate who had dewdrops in his eyes and made such awful faces. Such a thing did not generally occur in heaven, where all were good and quiet. But just then St. James came along and, on seeing the crying angel, he spoke pleasantly to him, and finally took him up in his arms in order to comfort him. But a great surprise lay in store for the Saint; for it would have been easier for him to convert a thousand heathens than to quiet the little unruly fellow, who commenced kicking and wriggling, and made such a terrible outcry that the angels fluttered away in consternation. There stood the Saint with the child in his arms, and did not know what to do! At last he concluded to show the strange being to the Lord Himself, and went with the little one before His throne. Then the Lord Almighty smiled, and all the angels around His throne smiled, when they saw St. James, who certainly did not seem very well adapted for nursing children, and in whose arms little Hans, regardless of all surroundings, continued to roar unmercifully. But the merciful Lord opined that the greatest squallers often turned out the best men, and He ordered an angel to carry the little one back to dear earth.

And this was done. With mighty strokes of his pinions the heavenly messenger floated back to earth, which came nearer and nearer with its mountains, lakes, and rivers, and with the old, lifeworn town, and from out the town rose up the gabled roof of the parents' home with a cap of snow upon it.

The boy in the coffin opened his eyes, and with a cry of joy his mother pressed him to her heart. Among the boughs of the Christmas-tree there was a soft rustling and whispering.

Methinks the tree remembered that winter is only a deep sleep, and was dreaming of spring.

II.

The years of misery and war were over. In the streets of the old town, where only a few years ago the roll of the drum resounded, and where the plague, in deathly silence, had spread its black wings, there, the stork on the town-hall heard, to his great satisfaction, merry shouts of children,—the ringing laugh of peace. A group of boys chased each other noisily over the market-place, playing at war. War! which had desolated so many of their homes. Oh! the fresh, merry laughter of childhood! how like unto ivy it climbeth over all ruins and findeth at last the sunshine!

But there was one not amongst the noisy group, and that one was Hans. His parents perceived with anxiety that the little noisy child had grown into a silent, shy boy, who avoided the games of his comrades and dreamingly went his own way. For hours he sat in the garden on the bench near his mother's flowers, and gazed dreamingly at the busy bees and butterflies, or lay in the woods near by and stared up through the branches of the beech-trees at the blue sky.

"What are you thinking of?" his mother would ask at times; then he would start up like one awakened from sleep, the thread of whose dreams are broken by awaking. "He is ill," the mother would think, anxiously. But folks would shake their heads suspiciously when, on speaking to the boy, they received no other answer than a shy, questioning look. "There is something wanting," said some, with an unmistakable gesture. "He is a fool," murmured others.

Thus a boy fares who has peeped too early into Paradise. The children of his own age made fun of him, and poor Hans would have been quite forsaken if Liesel from next door had not taken his part. She was quite the opposite to him,—merry and high-spirited. Whilst he sat dreaming, she was romping about, singing and laughing. But the children kept together, and the parents thought they might some day be a pair. The boy's reserved nature vexed the father, and, being of the opinion that man's hand cannot learn too early to handle and knead the tough clay of existence, he apprenticed him to a potter, in the hope that time would change the character of his son. He was mistaken, however; the boy grew up a fine, handsome youth, but in character he remained the boy of former days. If he looked up from his work it was not in order to gaze, like other journeymen, after a young girl who maybe was tripping past; but to stare up at the sky, which shone so blue between the houses, or to follow with his eyes the great white clouds away,—who knows whither? In his free time he did not go like others to the market-place, but would mount the ramparts at the back of his parents' house and gaze into the valley below, where the river was bearing its silvery wavelets into the far distance. What might not be in the far distance? Far, far away yonder must be the place where the dream of his childhood was realized! How astonished, then, was his father, when one fine sunny spring morning his son stood before him, with knapsack and staff, in order to bid him farewell before setting out on his travels. Who would ever have thought he would want to travel! The father rejoiced in the belief that the son would seek work according to the custom of journeymen workmen, and gave him his blessing, and much good advice besides. But he hardly even heard the words and advice of his father; there was a singing in his ears and a mist before his eyes, so that he felt like one intoxicated. Yes, he was a fool! Nor did he see the tears his mother and Liesel were shedding at his departure: he only thought of that far-off land, of the dream of his childhood. What mattered to him their tears! He wanted only to travel to find his Eden. And he travelled. With each rising sun he arose and thought, "To-day you will find what you seek;" and when he laid himself down tired at night, he thought, "To-morrow I shall reach my goal;" and, happy in this thought, he would fall asleep. No mountain was too steep for him, no path too stony, no forest too dense; he thought of his Eden, and minded not the thorns that tore his flesh. Yes, he was a fool!

Far behind him, forgotten, lay his home in the dim distance!

No living creature could tell him where his Paradise lay! The birds of the forest went on with their song; the deer gazed at him astonished; the brooks babbled on monotonously and sought the way to the ocean. People he asked only laughed, and they looked back at the strange lad, shaking their heads.

Quickly the time flew by; the spring faded, summer and autumn passed, and still he wandered on. His path, that once lay before him green and fair, was now covered with snow. He, however, heeded it not, and journeyed on. It must come at last, the long-sought goal! At last he reached a mighty snow-covered mountain range, so mighty that he said to himself, "Beyond this it must surely lie," and in glad hope passed forward. A whole day he ascended over snow and ice: his feet were sore and bruised, and he was shivering from the cold, and yet no hut was to be seen that might offer him shelter. The sun went down in crimson behind the ice-armored mountains, leaving behind a bitter coldness, so great that the stars in the heavens shivered with frost.

Then it occurred to tired Hans that it was Christmas, and for the first time on his journey he thought for a long while of home, where the Christmas-tree was now lighting up the warm room, and the dear ones were assembling around it. But what mattered the Christmas-tree to him; he was seeking Paradise!

Suddenly he saw on the roadside an old man. He was sitting on his bundle, and leaning his head on his hands. He must have been very old, for his face was furrowed like the bark of an oak, and his snowy beard hung nearly to the ground.

Then tired Hans rejoiced, greeted him, and asked how far it might be to the nearest habitation of man.

"To-day you can no longer reach it," replied the old man. "Whither are you journeying?"

"I seek Paradise," answered Hans: "nearly a year have I wandered over the earth, and yet have not found it."

Thereupon the old man arose, laid his hands upon Hans's shoulder, and said, "Turn back and go home! I have wandered for more than a thousand years on earth, and sought Paradise, and have not found it. Know, then, I am Ahasuerus, doomed to everlasting wandering as a penance. Wherever I go I am persecuted; where I knock the gate is locked; and nowhere have I a home. Stones are my bed, and my bundle is my pillow. Go, poor fool! return to the place of your birth. There, some day, they will dig a grave for you, wherein you may sleep peacefully. Go back to your home, where a Christmas-tree is lit up for you, and where you are loved, and leave to me all wandering and seeking: to me, the poor, old, accursed man!"

Then Hans was very sad: he threw down his bundle, sat down in the snow, and wept bitterly. However, he was so tired from the long journey that he soon forgot all his misery, and fell into a deep slumber. The old man spread his cloak over him to protect him from the cold, and then listened to the deep-drawn breathing of precious sleep, that drowns all cares. The youth lying there could sleep, and die, and forget! but he himself must keep awake, and live, and wander!

Upon the face of Hans a smile was playing; he was dreaming! Did he see the long-sought Paradise? He saw in his dream a house with snow-covered gable and little windows; a small house, closely encircled by other houses, a garden in front. In a room inside sat his parents round a cheerful fire. The spinning-wheel whizzed, and the cat purred in comfort in front of the fire. Softly there fell, now and again, a needle from the Christmas-tree. A resinous, pine-tree odor filled the room. From the next house a clear, maiden's voice was singing the old, old Christmas carol,—

"A rose has bloomed
From a tender root,
Our fathers have sung:
Out of Jesse it came."

And the crackling of the fire, the whizzing of the spinning-wheel, and the maiden's song seemed to the dreamer fairer than a thousand Edens. An indescribable homesickness overcame him.

When he awoke, the east was radiant with the blush of morning. He sprang up and seized his staff. Scales seemed to fall from his eyes. "Home, home!" a thousand voices seemed to echo within him.

But up the mountains, outlined by the red of the morn, he saw the old man wandering on his comfortless path.

———————————————————————————

A Yarn Spun by a Yankee.

"A white-haired, thin-visaged, weather-worn old gentleman in a blue, Quaker-cut coat."

Hawthorne.

A TALE OF A TURKEY.

I.

The shutters of a little spur of warehouses which breaks out into mountainous stores and open valleys of streets around the corner, but which itself overlooks no fairer view than a narrow, muddy alley of a thoroughfare scarcely broad enough to admit two drays abreast, and, by actual measurement,—taken with persistent diligence by the adjacent office boys,—just two running-jumps from gutter to gutter; the shutters of this, in its own eyes, important little trade centre, were up, and a great clattering they had made in getting up on a clear, tingling night before Christmas, eighteen hundred and—no matter what.

The porters had come out in their faded greatcoats, bandaged right and left in woolly mufflers, and more than usually clumsy in padded gloves, and had been bitten and tossed about by the wind with such unbecoming violence that even a porter felt it necessary to hurry and bustle. Taking the shutters by assault from the foe's embraces, they had thumped, and banged, and hammered, and scolded them into place, and, in undignified haste, had betaken themselves, steaming warm breath through their fingers, into their proper and respective places by the counting-house fire.

The magic—so it seemed in its effects—tolling of a deep-toned bell in the neighborhood would not allow them to doze long in their warm nooks, but, like the jealous monster in the fairy-tale, kept its captives always going, going, going, for its sixth stroke had not died away before they began to appear again, this time with the addition of fur hats and little dinner-baskets, and with no perceptible noses—unless the existence of watery eyes above their mufflers argued the missing features to be in their proper places below—and with an accelerated gait—also an act of enchantment.

William, of No. 6, bawled as loud as his worsted gag would permit across the street (so termed by a figure of rhetoric) to James, of No. 7:

"Hello, Jim! Cold as blazes, ain't it?"

James, of No. 7, assenting, Thomas, of No. 4, would like to know "How blazes can be cold, now?"

William, of No. 6, would say "as thunder," if that would suit him any better; and as it appeared to do so they, with half a dozen others, breasted the wind and trudged out into the blustery streets beyond.

The merchants, too, had locked their doors, and tried their knobs, and looked up at the faces of their stores as if to say, "Merry Christmas to you, and I wish you a pleasant day to-morrow!" but in reality to see that all was fast, and perchance to indulge in a comfortable survey of their snug little properties—and the complacent tread with which they followed the porters gives color to the suspicion—and draw from it momentum for the enjoyment of the morrow's holiday.

The shutters, then, were up—stop, not all up! One, as you may see by the shaft of gas-light that has just fallen across the pavement near the top of the court, is still down.

The little square window through which the light eddies on the bricks is supported on either side by a heavy door, and all three, the two doors and the window, are in turn crowned and anointed on the head, as it were, by a very bold sign containing very brazen—in every sense of the word—letters which announced pompously, like some servants of similar metallic qualities, the name of their master.

Emanuel Griffin—the tongue uncontrollably adds Esquire—was the name, and there, if you had looked through the window, in a deep funnel of a room, at a desk near the fire, head behind the open leaves of a ledger, and feet beneath the warm recesses of the stove, sat its possessor.

Outside the railing which formed a barrier between Emanuel Griffin, Esq., and the business world, and encompassed with a less elaborate railing, sat, on a high stool in a cold corner, the little, blackish-green (perhaps the color gas-light imparts to faded black) clerk of Emanuel Griffin, Esq. Whether David Dubbs, such was he called, derived the power of writing from his mouth; or whether the gentle excitation of moving his lips over toothless gums assisted thought; or whether, as some said, he chewed tobacco, a position which nobody ever held long, as nobody ever proved him to have expectorated during his whole life; his mouth—always closed—moved up and down, up and down, with the motion of his pen. Hair he had none, that is, none to speak of; there were some few isolated white locks behind his ears and at the back of his head, but he made no pretensions to have any, and openly acknowledged himself bald—and very candid of him it was to do so.

Chroniclers have told us how, after fierce battles that have raged from dawn till nightfall, the moon has come calmly up from the horizon and shone peacefully and serenely over the field of strife and death. So arose a beneficent smile ever and anon over the wrinkled and careworn face of the old clerk; but still he wrote on, Faithful Dave! and if pleasant thoughts swept through him they avoided the business that occupied his hands and did not interrupt it.

They had long sat in quietness, only broken by the noise of turning leaves and crackling coals,—but, in truth, if David Dubbs's eye, in its course to and from the clock, had not, like the world, worked silently on its axis, there must have been continual creaking—when a noise like the name of David emanated from the ledger, and following it—for it was near-sighted—the head of Emanuel Griffin, Esq., lifted itself to an erect posture and repeated in a less muffled tone, "David!"

"Yes, sir," answered the old clerk, in a weak little voice, and climbing down to the floor from his perch.

"You may lock up, David. Ten thousand and odd. Ten thousand's a good year, David; a very good year. Very—good—indeed! But go and lock up," and then Mr. Griffin took a glance at the clock. "Half-past six! Why it's surprising how time does fly, and Christmas Eve, too. Well, well! But hurry up with the shutters, David, and we shan't be long——"

Before Mr. Griffin had fully delivered himself of these remarks the little person of David Dubbs was out in the cold, was in and out among the screws on the door, had put up the shutters, and simultaneously with the last word stood in the half-opened door and, all unseen by his employer, waved his hand to some one at the corner of the court. He then walked as quickly as his little, bent legs—parabolic were they in outline, but, as this is not a geometric treatise, it is of no particular consequence—would permit him up the long aisle in the centre of the room, and sent off timid little echoes of his steps to ramble away among the bales of crockery—for it was crockery that Emanuel Griffin, Esq., dealt in—and rattle among the piles of plates.

Having reached again his little cage of an office, he took down from its accustomed peg an old, threadbare coat, and, with much exertion and outstretching of arms, finally got it on, turned up the collar, tied about his ears a not very robust scarf, and laid thereon, as the copestone of his apparel, a dingy high hat that had undergone, in point of nap, as many reverses as its wearer in point of fortune. Thus attired, he tipped his hat to his employer, all ready, like himself, to depart, and started out.

Before he reached the door, a cry from Mr. Griffin arrested him, and he came hastily back; for, although it would have required a thumbscrew to have made him confess it, yet he had all day long looked forward to the time of parting, when he half expected Emanuel Griffin, Esq., contrary to his custom though it was, would offer him some little gift out of the increased profits of a business he had done no little to advance. But no such design had Mr. Griffin conceived, or if he had it was very soon suppressed as entirely unworthy of a man of purely business habits, and all he had to say was,—

"I know, David, there is something I was to have told you to do. Mrs. Griffin impressed it on me this morning, but,"—here he stood thinking for a moment,—"no matter," he resumed. "I guess it was nothing very important, so good-by, David, and a—good-by!" He was going to say "and a merry Christmas;" but for a man of purely business habits to unbend so far and become cheerful—why, it's subversive of all business discipline, and so he thought to himself.

David, doubly disappointed, turned and passed out, and his old eyes must have been extremely sensitive to the wind, for they ran with something very like tears that he wiped away with his glove as he muttered,—

"So, no Christmas, after all. Poor girls! Poor girls!" Mr. Griffin was not long behind his faithful old clerk. He extinguished the lights with great care, and then, with the key in his hand, felt his way to the door, banged it after him, and locked it with the satisfaction of a miser over a casket of treasures. His journey home led him to the opposite end of the court from that which David had passed through, and he therefore did not overtake him.

And if he had, would this hard, business-encrusted heart have been less cold than the bitter winds that assailed it? Would the sight which made David Dubbs forget the fierceness of night have penetrated the chilly place where it rested and warmed it in pitying activity? Would the tender impulses, which the unsifted morals of barter extinguish, as they extinguish much of the nobility in man, have enkindled anew and brightened this misery? Not if dollars would have done it; nay, not if even a word would have done it, would Emanuel Griffin have relaxed from the demeanor which purely business habits imposed upon him. He felt it due to his position in business society to maintain rigidly its maxims, the chief of which, "Do unto others as they would do unto you, if they could," he practised to the letter.

II.

Poor David Dubbs! Oh, the long time it seemed since boon companions had smitten him on the back and cried, "Bravo, Dave Dubbs! Bravo, old fellow!" to his little songs, or encouraged him by such exclamations as "Dave Dubbs can't be beat at a ballad!" Oh, the long, long time ago! But to proceed. As David Dubbs met the ambushed winds that leaped upon him at the corner of the court, he also met the person to whom he had waved his hand from the store-door. If you had looked for the stature of a man you would have been doubly mistaken,—first in sex, next in size. It was neither a man nor a woman. There, in a blustery doorway, shaking with cold, but ever on the alert, crouched a little girl. She wore a knitted hood, and out of it fell overflowing curls; but her poor, attenuated little body was ill-assorted with plenty of any kind, and the wealth of curls mocked the poverty of her clothes. A patched shawl affected to protect her poor little shoulders, and a calico dress flapped coldly about her legs. As David turned the corner she arose, and, for all her stiffness and shivering, exclaimed, cheerily, "A merry Christmas, father!" and reached to kiss him.

He took her in his arms—she was very, very slight—and lifted her to his lips, and then, throwing one side of his own scanty coat about her and holding it there with an affectionate hug, he said, "Come, come, little daughter, it's too bleak for a little body like you to be out. It's cruel, cruel, but I dared not tell him it was so late. What does he know or care for my poor little faithful, Loving Scout?"

"Your Scout couldn't miss Christmas Eve, father, if it was ever so cold."

"And does she ever miss? No, no, she's a dutiful Scout, winter and summer, rain and shine, morning and night, and what should I ever do without her!"

So, talking and fighting the wind by turns, they walked on, the bent and shuffling old man and his Little Scout, as he had named her and as they all affectionately called her, through dark streets where, ever and anon, a car or belated dray shivered by, as if the cold had touched even its insensibility, and made the tracks resound and the paving blocks rattle in the clear air; through deep cisterns of streets, between lofty stone banks—as stern almost as their governing boards, for, although boards are chiefly wooden, a supplication will quickly petrify them; through rows of illuminated stores like walls of Arabian Night visions, with traceries of frost on their windows richer in design than the gems within them; through clustering crowds that entered or left continually the swinging doors of saloons and hotels; past waiting carriages; past swearing men; past laughing ladies, and past beggars, wearier, and colder, and lonelier than themselves. So they travelled, scarcely heeding what they saw in their speed until, on the margin of all the din, by a turn through a dark street, they reached a darker alley, and, passing down it, at last stopped before their own homely door.

The building had once been a warehouse,—David liked it the better for that, he said. "Why, all my life has been spent in trade, and, you see, I've sort a become attached to anything that smacks of it, though I've little reason to feel so, the Lord knows!" he would exclaim to his friends. Up above, over a long door in the top story—you can scarcely make it out in the uncertain light—jutted a weather-beaten crane, with a long disused pulley dangling at its point, cracked, and rusted, and abandoned, and no less cracked and abandoned, shot out from the second floor a moss-covered platform that had been intended for the reception of bales of stuffs that had never arrived. The mortar had, here and there, been wrenched from between the bricks by savage weather and age, and the doors, too, had shrunk before their united malignity. How such a house had drifted to such a locality is unaccountable, unless—as is often the case—some navigator of real estate had thought he descried a port, where was only a shoal that left his venture high and dry among newer and costlier craft.

However, the nearest approach it had made in the last twenty years or so—so David said—to fulfilling its commercial place in the world was in opening its doors to a gentleman in the carpentering line. This gentleman, Mr. Jacob Tripple by name, occupied the ground floor, and all around it were scattered evidences, in the shape of window-frames, and wooden-horses, and props, and old lumber, of a thriving business. He, with all his men, had departed long ago and left the place dark, and still, and cold.

It had lain in this stupor of silence for more than an hour, waiting against hope to be resuscitated by any stray echoes that should drop in from the neighboring hubbub and waken it up, when it caught among its bleak angles the cheery voice of David's Little Scout, and revived—as some old men do under the charm of gentle words—to a more respectable opinion of itself. So immediately it seemed refreshed, that if it were possible for such a decrepit—not to say inanimate—old structure as that even metaphorically to prick up its ears, it metaphorically did as the sound of Dolly's—her proper name—cheery welcome home echoed round it.

"Here we are once more, father," she cried, breaking away from him to have the door open when he plodded up to it. "Once more, and a welcome home, and a merry Christmas to you!"

"Always on duty, Little Scout! Always on duty!" he called after her. (The wind was keen and drew water to his eyes again, and again he brushed it away.) "Always on duty," he went on repeating, with a doleful effort at cheerfulness.

She was up-stairs by that time, and, opening the door above, had called in, "Here's father!" then ran back to meet him, which she did at the door below.

What these unusual proceedings meant, David Dubbs might have guessed or might have known traditionally, they being of an annual nature, but whether he did or not, or whether his ignorance was also traditional, he gave no sign, and walked feebly up-stairs, guided by the Little Scout, just as if it were not Christmas Eve at all.

What the proceedings did mean was that a steaming pot of coffee at the given signal was lifted from its warm corner and tilted into a cup that held a conspicuous place at the head of a little white spread table. On its right hand sat, in the position of an honored and seldom present guest, a juicy-complexioned, but not corpulent beefsteak; opposite to it, inviting death by explosion, rested a bowl full of steaming potatoes in their native jackets, and the centre was fully occupied by a huge loaf with a large family of slices.

Around this collation—aroused by the signal, for they had been idly waiting before—moved two pairs of hands with loving attention. The cloth was resmoothed, the knives and forks straightened, a brace of mealy potatoes was emptied on the two plates that awaited them, and at last a ruddy slice of beefsteak was deposited beside and oozed through them its savoriness. This last climax was reached just as the door opened, and the two pairs of hands speedily transferred themselves to the duty—no very arduous one—of helping David and Dolly out of their wraps.

And then, with many caresses and kisses and cries of "Take this side, father, where the coals are bright!" or "Put your feet here and get them good and warm, poor Little Scout!" then, when thick flying questions and travellings to the one end of the room for things that were not wanted, and excursions to the other end of the room for things that were wanted; when the chairs were drawn up; when the grateful old man and his little daughter, with those tender hands over their mouths to stifle the gratitude they struggled to utter, were duly seated at the table, and when the kettle was singing its approval in the corner, then, only,—when all these preliminaries were gone through with,—did the possessors of the hands that devised them seat themselves on a low wooden settee opposite the table and enjoy the zest and delight they had ministered to.

Good nature and tender hearts, pale faces and cheerful eyes, honest red hands and neatly bound-up hair have never been faithfully reproduced in a state of print and paper, much less in imagination, and, indeed, how can anything so buxom and comely, even if the plainest in dress, be expected to be? It is, therefore, needless to say that the twin daughters of David, namely, Molly and Polly Dubbs, being all that is here set down, should have been seen in all their kindliness to be truly known, and no other form of introduction would do them full justice.

Molly was the counterpart of Polly in all respects save height. She was a very little taller than Polly, and a fortunate thing it had been for all concerned that she was so. Else, consider the vexation of the measles and other diseases essential to youth. Why, in their quandary which to begin on, they almost missed the twins altogether as it was. Consider the complexity of young lovers who should pour into the ears of Polly passionate adjectives intended solely to captivate the heart of Molly; and, most important of all, consider the conflict of choice which would have disquieted the soul of Mr. Jacob Tripple and at last driven him to the alternatives of suicide or bigamy.

But all these dangers had been averted by the provisions of Nature, and the twins, who had supped, for economic reasons, earlier in the evening, sat beaming on while David and little Dolly heartily devoured the supper.

David, looking up now for the first time, in the interval of a mouthful swallowed and a mouthful threatened, espied a bowery wreath of holly that hung around a picture of General Washington in the act of crossing a dark, green river Delaware in a court dress of red and breeches of yellow, surrounded on all sides by ice and officers in rainbow uniforms, and, as this was the only adornment of a rather bare room, it is no wonder it caught his eye.

"Why, who's been a-brightening up the gen'ral so Christmas-like?" he exclaimed.

"We did, father! Leastwise it was Polly's present," said Molly.

"And who may be a-sending presents to Polly now?" asked David, with a twinkle in his eye that had seen better days but none kindlier. "It wasn't young Cuffy over at the baker's, nor Jake Tripple, now, was it?"

He looked at Polly for an answer, whereat she stretched her arm along the back of the settee and let fall her hand on Molly's shoulder with a punch which was intended as punishment for the giggles her sister struggled to confine in her mouth with both hands; but which, in spite of her, bubbled over and attacked David, and then, with a blush, Polly muttered,—

"It wasn't young Cuffy at all, and I hate his loafy, little face, and I hate——"

"Not Jacob Tripple! No, no, not good Jake Tripple?" said David, reprovingly.

"I didn't say that, father!" she exclaimed. "He's your good old friend, and how could I hate him? He came in just before leaving for the day, and asked for you—what, made him think you were home I can't tell, for it was long before your time—and asked for you, and left the wreath for—for—me."

The hem of her long checkered apron then needed close scrutiny and folding for some unknown purpose, and this duty diverted her thoughts from the subject, but she turned to Dolly, who enjoyed this banter in her own quiet little way, which seldom rippled into a loud laugh, for her own quiet little face was too pale and too pinched to invite such freebooters. "Come, come, Little Scout," she said. "Is she warm now, and were the rations good, and did she meet Kriss Kingle on his cold journey (with a caress of her pale little cheeks) with heaps of warm dresses, and heaps of pretty dolls, and heaps of sweetmeats too big to carry himself, so he asked her to carry some home to help him! Did she? (with another caress.) And would our Little Scout be sorry if he didn't come himself to look after them and——"

"Ah, that reminds me!" said David, quite audibly for him, and rising from the table with knife and fork still in hand.

"What reminds you, father?" asked the twins, in chorus.

"Why, coming home!" said David, not very intelligibly.

"What coming home?" again from the chorus, in expectant attitude.

"Why, Tom, I told you!" which he hadn't done at all, but as by this time he was deep in the cupboard, where his overcoat hung, and as his voice was a little more muffled than usual, it was useless to argue the point, so the chorus loudly exclaimed,—

"Tom?"

"Yes, yes, yes!" from David, faintly and rather testily, as he had groped through his old coat, and had successively dropped the knife and fork, reeking with gravy, into the inside and outside pockets.

"To be sure! Tom coming home and I clean forgot it, what with the cold and the surprises," he said again, emerging with the knife and fork in one hand and a letter in the other. "Here it is. He'll be home to-morrow, he says, God willin', and eat our turkey with us. Poor Tom, poor boy! He's been away so long he's forgot Griffin and hard times, or he wouldn't say that!"

"Tom! Be home! and to-morrow?"—interruption of chorus as it reaches for the letter, opens and reads it aloud—Dolly being lifted in the sturdy arms of Molly to look over.

David, meanwhile, overcome by the toothsomeness of beefsteak, falls to again, while the others dance a sort of fandango, and turn up the rag carpet, and rattle the dishes on the dresser, and lift

Dolly high in the air to the improvised tune of "Tom's coming home! Tom's coming home! Tom's coming home to-morrow!"

"It's another mouth to feed, but it's hard to wish the poor boy back to Californy again," huskily said David; then he exclaimed, as the noise increased, "Hey dey! Why, you'll spill the coffee next, and cave in the walls, too, in a minute, and then there'll be no home for Tom to come to!"

This was good humoredly added as the final swing was given to the dance, which brought the twins holding Dolly aloft in their arms laughing and panting on the settee.

"But tell us, father, is he coming home for good? He don't say so in the letter," asked Dolly, and all leaned forward to hear his answer.

"Coming home for good?" mused David. "Yes, he's coming home for good, I hope; but I'm fearful he'll find little beside the good in his sisters' hearts."

"Poor Tom," said Dolly, with far-away eyes, "he's had a weary life of it in the mines, I guess, poor fellow."

"Yes, yes," said David, "and that's what makes it harder that we can't greet him with a good Christmas to-morrow. Well, well, it'll be a delight to see my poor boy again, hard times or no hard times, and we'll be as cheerful as we can be and are now, thanks to my good girls," and here he arose from the table, and, seating himself at the fire, opened a morning paper that he had found in the waste-basket in Mr. Griffin's counting-house (and very worthless it must have been to be found there!) in which, through the kind offices of a massive old pair of spectacles, he was soon absorbed.

And now, while the Little Scout—in fulfilment of her established character—plays the spy on sundry crumbs that slink from notice under the table, and while the twins, too busy to talk, wash the dishes and dispose them in a glistening row along the dresser, and, while David opens the paper and plods up and down it, column by column, like a ploughman furrow by furrow up and down a field, and with almost as much toil; and while the ancient clock on the shelf over the stove and under the motley General Washington ticks loud enough to be heard above the clinking dishes and simmering kettle; and while the table, divested of its cloth and exhibiting a stained and blistered old back, is glad enough to avoid attention by being stowed away in the corner; while the pleasant spirits of domesticity that come only at the call of good men, and good wives, and good sons, and good daughters, but resist the imperious beckonings of the wealthiest hands, and wing on over their roofs to lowlier, and scantier, and purer habitations—while the pleasant spirits of domesticity and kindliness throng invisibly into the room, and David Dubbs reads stray scraps from his paper to his daughters, grouped near the fire at his feet, we must softly withdraw and leave them to the care of coming Christmas dreams.

III.

Christmas morning had opened brightly with David Dubbs. The sun, preceded down the court by hustling winds that knocked at every citizen's door and demanded admittance for their oncoming master, had left at each house a gift of golden cheerfulness. The sky above was so blithe and blue that it smiled down at even so insignificant a crack as David Dubbs's court must have appeared to it; and the cold was a jolly and snappish cold.

The twins and David's Little Scout were as merry as the Christmas chimes they lingered and listened to, and not the daintiest dinner that Mr. Cuffy (and that gentleman held the subject somewhat in mind, too, on Polly's account) could have delivered at their door would have added one jot of happiness to their abundance. David's poor old back bent under the stress of poverty that would permit him no indulgences for them—all the more dear on that day; but, used to loving self-denial, they never missed what they so little desired, and so far were they from giving it a thought, that if David had spoken out what he so wilfully turned over and over in his mind, that would have given them far more pain and anxiety. Mr. Tripple was early in his shop, presumptively to attend to some forgotten duties, but, as he did not pay very active attention to anything but carefully tying up a square box in white paper, and as he did pay very active attention to what went on up-stairs, at the same time exhibiting no hurry to get home to dinner, David, who had, towards noon, gone around the corner with Polly to make some little purchases of groceries before the stores closed, dropped in on his way back and invited Mr. Tripple up-stairs. Mr. Tripple at first firmly refused, and said, "Very much obliged, Dave, but couldn't think of it. Indeed not. They'd 'spect me at home, ye know, Dave." Whereupon Miss Polly added her entreaties, and said he needn't expect anything very much, but if he would walk up they would be very happy to have him. Mr. Tripple would have walked up—and, indeed, wanted very much to walk up—at first, but his extreme awkwardness, aggravated by holiday clothes of a tight cut and by a paper collar bent above his coat like a scimetar, and almost as sharp and glistening as that weapon, impelled him to do violence to his wishes in order to appear calm—under her eyes—and to deceive them politely as to his real desire. But now, lured on by the siren voice of Polly, he consented to go up "a little while" (which meant all the afternoon), and taking the white box under his arm he locked the shop-door and followed them up the creaking stairs.

Arrived in the room and relieved of hat and coat, Mr. Tripple bowed mysteriously to Dolly, and, intrusting her with the box, whispered,—"Go and hand that to sister Polly, little un." Polly, receiving it from her, exclaimed in surprise,—

"For me, Mr. Tripple?"

"Yes, miss," he replied, growing red and smiling broadly, "a little something for Christmas, that's all."

Polly opened the box and extracted a pasteboard plane with some artificial shavings pasted upon it, which, when lifted apart, discovered a heap of sweetmeats. Dolly and Molly, looking on, exclaimed, "Why, Mr. Tripple, what a surprise!" and Polly blushingly added, "So very unexpected!"

Mr. Tripple grew redder and nervously crossed his legs, saying, "I thought 'twould be kind a appropriate to the trade, you know, and so I just fetched it up, and——"

Then Polly, seeing his embarrassment, called on David and the rest to come and help themselves, and there was good humor and laughing until the twins darted away to got dinner, which was soon prepared, for there was little enough to get, and all invited to sit up to the table.

All were duly in their places, and David had, in accordance with Christmas custom, offered grace. Mr. Tripple and the girls were slowly raising their bowed heads, when a loud knock announced a visitor, and hastened the raising of heads to an unseemly hurry.

"Tom!" all exclaimed.

Molly hurried down-stairs, and the rest rushed to the stair-landing, where, in a moment, they received, not Tom, but a large, square basket that emitted a very fragrant smell of roasted fowl, in the arms of the returning Molly. Once in the room, the lid was off in a twinkling, and out came a sizable plate, enveloped in dainty, clean napkins, which, being removed in layers, exhibited, in all its brown deliciousness, a huge turkey, just done to a turn.

The party gathered around in pleased wonder, and as Molly threw the napkins into the basket a card fell on the floor. She picked it up and, astonished, read, "Emanuel Griffin."

"What!" said David, snatching it and reading it aloud to himself, "Emanuel Griffin. So it is, and no mistake!" and then he burst out, "Hurrah! hurrah for Griffin! I knew he couldn't forget us this year!" His poor old face was almost young again, and his voice,— why, it could actually be heard as he ran on: "Why, there never was such a year for the china trade, Tripple, and how could he forget me? Jacob Tripple, your hand! A kiss, Little Scout! Why, your old father's 'most young again, and his good girls shall dine like other good girls, after all! How very thoughtful of Griffin to send it in the nick of time, too. Come, sit up again before it gets cold, and I wish we had something as hot to drink Griffin's health in. Why, I believe I could sing a song again if we had something hot. I do, indeed!"

So he ran on in his childish delight at the thought of being remembered, and at the far more grateful thought that his beloved daughters were to share the gift with him.

When he had ceased, all turned to Molly and asked in one breath who had left it. When the clamor slackened, she replied, "Why, young Cuffy from the baker's, and all he said was, 'David Dubbs,—to be sent—card inside,' and then kissing his hand, and crying 'Love to her,' meaning I don't know who," with a smirk at Polly, "he jumped aboard his wagon and flew away down the court."

Never was a turkey enjoyed so much, and never had a turkey better deserved it.

Mr. Tripple grew bland and talkative under its juicy influence. He even winked at Polly occasionally, and one time actually chucked her under the chin. She sat next to him, remarking that if he had his way she should live forever on turkey and sugar-plums. David ventured to say that that course of diet would be pretty indigestive, whereupon Mr. Tripple fondly suggested, as he gazed into her eyes, "How would love do for a substitute, then?" implying that "his way" would supply that abstract edible in equally large doses.

David dryly added "Starvation," and thereupon Polly covered her face with her hands, but left open a laughing eye at Molly, and Mr. Tripple looked boldly around the board as a man who had said a very bright thing indeed, after which survey he broke out into a not very comfortable laugh. All the rest laughed, too, then, and such good humor prevailed that nothing seemed amiss, and Mr. Tripple's inexperience was kindly overlooked.

But now the turkey was fast becoming skeletonized, and the good company was fast becoming the reverse. The jollity was increasing and the serious intentions of Mr. Tripple were impending and ready to fall into open profession on the slightest encouragement. The Little Scout's pinched and pale face—sweet and uncomplaining, even through hunger and want—smiled gently and less sadly as it leaned in Molly's arms, and, looking up, she said,—

"Poor father! How quiet you were last night when we were walking home. I knew you were thinking about to-day and the poor dinner.

How kind it was of good Mr. Griffin. I'd like to thank him myself, father!"

"And so you shall, Little Scout," said David, gayly, bending over and kissing her with boyish contempt of aged bones; "and so you shall, and I make no doubt he'll be glad to see you, too, Deary."

The clock in a neighboring steeple, simultaneously with its ancient kinsman on the shelf, and followed by incoming echoes of a score of others, struck one; but the company little heeded that, and the conviviality was far from diminishing when another summons rattled the street door, and again all exclaimed "There's Tom!" and crowded to the landing as before.

Polly this time tripped down and came back in a moment with only a letter, saying,—

"A young man, father, with this letter for Mr. Griffin. It's addressed to his store, but he said it was important, and, knowing you lived here, he depended on you to deliver it at once."

"Has he gone?" said David, grasping it.

"Yes, father," replied Polly, "right off."

Here was a pitiable state of affairs indeed. David Dubbs, aroused from the joyful celebration of his Christmas dinner and from the midst of this cosey party and sent off across the river to his master's house with a miserable letter and by a miserable young man (and if delivering letters when every other well-intentioned man is eating his turkey isn't miserable, why what is it?). Sent off on a graceless errand for nothing, perhaps. But his kind employer, who had done so much for his comfort and joy that very day, must not suffer by his neglect, and off he must post; that was imperative. Mr. Tripple offered his services when David had started down-stairs, and when there was no chance of his turning back, but David said, "No, no, Tripple; you just stay and keep the girls company till I get back, and that'll be enough for you to attend to. Good-by, girls. Good-by, Little Scout; if it wasn't so cold, she should go too." And off he trudged, as patient, and cheerful, and proud of his master's attention and of his mission, too, now he had fully set out, as many a younger and better dressed man would have been.

IV.

When Emanuel Griffin, Esq., leaving the dark little street wherein stood his warehouse and wherein very much of his life and very little of his money was spent—which latter fact had, however, no merely local application but was of a general nature—when, to resume, Emanuel Griffin, Esq., buttoning up his overcoat and, leaving the dark little street, turned the next corner among the mountainous stores and looked vexedly around for a car to bear him to his home across the river, and rattled his keys in his pocket, and nearly hummed a tune in his impatience, suddenly, as the car appeared like a new planet, and with the easy-going motions of a planet in its ascent had nearly reached him—suddenly a thought of something forgotten flashed through his mind, and the violence of its reaction turned him completely around and sent him in a precipitous hurry in the opposite direction, namely, in that which David Dubbs and his little daughter had pursued but a short time before.

"Pshaw!" he muttered, and looked as if he would like to add something a great deal stronger. "That's what I forgot to tell David; but Mrs. G. 'll never forget it, nor forgive it, either, if I don't attend to it before I get home." So he turned up his collar, and rubbed his ears, and hurried on to keep warm.

His destination proved to be a fancy bakery in the neighborhood of David Dubbs's house. The pavement in front of it at that hour and season, owing to holiday orders, was sending up warm steam from the oven beneath, and a fragrant and appetizing smell of hot bread and browning cakes pervaded the street. It was a large establishment of the kind, and besides its legitimate line of bread-baking, took charge of the cooking and preparing of dinners for ladies of limited domestic conveniences in fashionable life. Heedless of the delicious scents which had attracted several men with greedy eyes to linger at the window and devour in fancy—a process which left them hungrier than ever—the heaps of loaves and cakes on the counter within; heedless of the supplicating looks the men turned on him, and of the confidential attempts of one or two at a begging whisper (but his hurry was in nowise chargeable with that inattention); heedless of everything but finishing his errand and getting home, Mr. Griffin pushed through the crowd in the store, and, reaching the counter, beckoned to a light-haired, light-eyed, and red-cheeked youth, in a blue tie and black waistcoat that, through constant friction with loaves and flour-barrels, had become of a light pepper-and-salt pattern, and hurriedly said,—

"I want a turkey, Cuffy, of about fifteen or twenty pounds, cooked and sent to my house by one o'clock to-morrow."

"Can't do it, Mr. Griffin," said the young man, who knew him and had bowed as he came up.

"Can't do what?" exclaimed Mr. Griffin, with surprise and dismay.

"Can't send it out," returned the young man, firmly.

"Oh!" said Mr. Griffin, relieved; "I thought you meant that you couldn't prepare it!"

"No, sir," commenced the young man. "You see, sir, Mr. Griffin, it's so late in the day that all our teams is ordered fur to-morrow at that time, and so is our boys, but——"

"Well, I'll soon fix that, Cuffy," said Mr. Griffin, opening his coat and taking out a card. "There, just pin that on the turkey when it is ready, and carry it over here to Dubbs's—David Dubbs is my clerk. He will understand the card, and bring the turkey out to my house. I shouldn't be so particular about it if Mrs. Griffin had not impressed it on me this morning. I almost forgot it, too."

Then asking the price, and answering,—

"That is very high, Cuffy;" to which that young man replied,—

"I know it is, sir, Mr. Griffin, but then, you see, the demand is werry great, sir."

Mr. Griffin paid the bill and hurried out, took a car at the next corner, and, after a long, cold ride, got home to allay the anxiety of Mrs. Griffin by assuring her that the turkey was ordered, and would be sent home promptly to-morrow by David Dubbs.

Christmas morning was, among the Griffin household, which consisted of Mr. and Mrs. Griffin and a superannuated servant, a very busy morning indeed, for the reason that Mrs. Griffin had, according to annual custom, invited more guests to dine than she could conveniently provide for. Their house was a cottage in the suburbs, pretty enough in summer and no thanks to its mistress or the superannuated servant either, but to the unaided impulse of nature, which climbed, in the form of bowery vines, wherever a vine could find clinging room; but now, in the midst of winter, bright though the day was, the skeletons of so much green gayety looked bare, and inhospitable, and cold. The house was approached by a long path that started at the iron gate and led up to the porch. It was far from a large house, and looked inconvenient, and famished for paint, and it was no less inconvenient than it looked, a fact, indeed, which necessitated the purchase of a cooked turkey, for the oven was small, and the stove in the crazy little kitchen needed all the surface it could afford for the vegetables, oysters, and other viands which then only, throughout the year, it blazed and glowed under.

The morning wore on and twelve o'clock arrived. The big table in the little dining-room was duly dressed and adorned with Mrs. Griffin's miscellaneous silver; and after a heated debate between that lady and the Superannuated, it was decided that when the company were all in the parlor the dining-room door should be left open, and at the bottom of the table, which now projected against the door, an additional chair for Mr. Griffin should be inserted.

Mrs. Griffin said of course the company must squeeze in, but they understood all that, and were glad enough to get in by any means, to which Superannuated readily assented.

One o'clock, and now the company were all arrived. Mrs. Griffin was duly excused by Mr. Griffin, who received them, on the plea of domestic duties. They were mostly in the parlor, which contained, beside them, a set of red velvet furniture and a shining piano, on legs which emulated the unsteadiness of Superannuated's own, and which, in huskiness of voice, also resembled that person; a portrait of Mr. Griffin in rigid broadcloth, and a companion portrait of Mrs. Griffin in low neck and volumes of lace; and last, a very pimply-looking carpet, which seemed to suffer from a severe rash.

Mr. Griffin had occupied the space between the folding-doors as the company arrived and suavely—as suavely, by the way, as his wincing at the cost of it all would admit of—received, introduced, and seated them. The first arrival was a single gentleman, whom he saluted as Fred. He was short, and bald, and spasmodic,—so much so that his pantaloons were never straight, and his collar, through much moistening of its raspy edges, was soiled. After him, a lady and gentleman drove up to the gate in a carriage, and, alighting, the lady swept up the path, in a double sense, while her husband upbraided the driver for the muddy condition of the carriage, and then, loudly, "At ten, William!" To which William as loudly replied, "Can't do it, sir. Got another order; but I'll send you another man."

The gentleman answered more quietly, with a careful look at the house, where Mr. Griffin awaited him on the porch,—

"Very well, driver;" and also swept in, and was introduced to Fred as Mr. Abbert.

Now came a pair who walked, and were addressed and handed around by the host as "My dear friends, Mr. and Mrs. Dripps;" and then the volume of newcomers became quite abundant; so much so that a number of gentlemen with no apparent use for their hands were forced to lean about the hall and sit on the stairs, which they did up to the very top one. When the company had simmered down a good deal, and only a few very bold gentlemen ventured to launch remarks into the unanswering silence, and when everybody was wondering what everybody else was going to do next, and all were, as they reported the next day, "enjoying themselves immensely," there was a stir above stairs, a rustling of dresses, and then the gentlemen on the stairs, like a row of falling bricks, were driven down before the gracious smiles and bows of the transformed hostess.

Tripping down after them and falling at last into the extended arms of her husband—rather unsteady under the weight—while the stiffly polite gentlemen formed a compact crowd out to the door. Mrs. Griffin was led, with no little difficulty, through the seated guests, bestowing bows, and smiles, and "Glad to see you, my dear Mr. Dripps," and "How well you're looking, my dear Mrs. Abbert," and "Welcome, gentlemen," (whereat a murmur ran through the crowd and all shook their heads and tried to turn round and bow, but utterly failed,) and "Oh! here's my old Fred," and sundry other bewitching remarks that led the crowd of gentlemen to murmur again something like "Charming, be Gad!" and grow uneasy.

But now the bell was rung by Superannuated, who had duly inserted the chair, and Mr. Abbert, receiving the hostess from the arm of her husband and in turn delivering his smiling wife to Mr. Griffin, led off the throng to dinner.

When they arrived at the protruding table, by a preconcerted arrangement Mrs. Griffin handed Mr. Abbert to the one side and squeezed herself through the other—an action which was imitated by the rest of the company, who were finally seated close up to the door—all but Mr. Griffin, who was to occupy the extra chair, and, as he was already inside, and there was no other means of exit, he was obliged to pass through the kitchen and around the house. He soon appeared again through the front door and the dinner began.

Mrs. Griffin, who had long before left Superannuated to finish while she perfected her toilet, now rang the bell and, on her appearance, whispered in her ear. Superannuated whispered in her mistress's ear. Mrs. Griffin thereupon uttered a little cry and looked at Mr. Griffin. Mr. Griffin, in consternation, cried, "My dear!" and attempted to squeeze between the chairs, but failed. Then he looked wildly about him, and at last ran through the front door. He soon reappeared at the side of his fainting wife, who revived enough to say,—

"I shall never, never forgive you! Oh, the humiliation! the agony!" then fainted again.

"What is it?" "What's the matter?" "She's fainted!" and confused screams of the ladies came from all sides. Mrs. Dripps passed along her salts bottle. Mrs. Abbert held Mrs. Griffin's head, and Fred applied water. Under the strong influence of these restoratives she soon revived, and whispered to her husband something which caused him also to start and look despairingly at her.

She then said to him, loud enough for all to hear, "You must tell them it was your fault. Oh, the humiliation!" Here she burst out again, with her handkerchief to her eyes, and Mrs. Abbert soothingly said, "Oh, never mind him, my dear. I wouldn't mind him!" This was growing invidious, and all the gentlemen at the bottom of the table were looking scornfully at him.

He therefore said, in a loud voice,—

"The turkey has not arrived,—that is all."

"That is all," whimpered Mrs. Griffin, mockingly. "That is all, he says; and isn't it enough, sir, to have all your domestic failings exposed to the world?"

Mrs. Griffin alluded to cooking facilities, and grew very bitter, while "the world" simpered and exchanged looks.

Mr. Griffin then, in desperation, explained the whole matter,—how he had left the card for David Dubbs, and paid for the turkey, and come unsuspectingly home. "As," he added, "I have done year after year, for——"

Here Mrs. Griffin checked him with symptoms of another faint, and he stopped short.

Mr. Abbert then said it was all that rascally clerk, and he ought to be discharged at once.

"I know 'em," he added violently and with deeply implied wisdom, which, by the way, was the only species of wisdom he ever attained to. "I know 'em, Griffin!"

Mr. Fred was of a similar opinion, and even more violent in his denunciation of David, as he had set his heart on turkey, and the appetite died painfully within him.

All the ladies and gentlemen were of various opinions, but all concentrated their rage on the poor, innocent little clerk, and panted for his clerkly death. In the midst of all this commotion the door-bell rang, and intensified it twofold, for nobody could get through to the door but by going around the house. This Superannuated finally did, and brought back with her the identical little clerk,—the poor, agitated, and bowing little clerk who had unconsciously aroused all the indignation and tumult, whom sundry gentlemen at the lower end of the table had threatened with severe punishment if they ever caught sight of him, and who, now catching sight of him, were more than usually silent.

Mr. Griffin looked threateningly at him as, hat in hand, he walked up to him, presented a letter, and, in his faint voice, said,—

"A letter for you, sir, left for me to deliver."

He took it, and David continued tremulously to say,—

"And how can I thank you, sir, and madam," turning to Mrs. Griffin, "for the bounteous gift——"

"Gift?" exclaimed both in a breath; "what gift? Where is the turkey you brought? What gift? What gift?"

"Why, a splendid turkey, with your card kindly——"

This was received by the company with a volley of cries and calls, by a relapse on the part of Mrs. Griffin, and by the descent of Mr. Griffin's hand upon David's coat-collar, and finally by poor, frightened David's ejectment from the kitchen-door, harshly reproached by his employer as a thief and vagabond, and warned never to show his face in his store again.

"Be off, now!" he cried after him, "you ungrateful, deceitful old villain!" and then he slammed the door, and joined the hungry guests, to whom he declaimed at some length on the thanklessness of the lower classes.

Mrs. Griffin was quickly re-restored, this time to a state of injured perfection, and after the united apologies of herself and husband, and more abuse of poor, luckless David Dubbs, the company concluded with pretty bad grace to make the most of what had been prepared in the way of vegetables and side dishes, long ago cold. Mr. Griffin was mad, insulted, and hungry, and the contents of the letter he had received seemed to add very little warmth to the food, but a great deal to his anger, for he tore it up into very small pieces, as if it were David himself he was torturing, and, with a look the company did not consider very sociable, scattered it on the floor.

V.

The sky, as if presaging David Dubbs's misfortune, had grown overcast, and flung down spiteful little sallies of snow as he crossed the river on his way to Mr. Griffin's. The creaking of the bridge's huge timbers and the splitting ice below it made him shiver and pull his threadbare coat close about him and sacrifice his old hands to the wind to save his freezing ears. The same scarf bound them as the night before, but an icy gale like that which swept from the open river would have frozen through arctic furs. Notwithstanding all this, his spirits were lighter than usual. The scene he had left at home floated on before his eyes, and transfused itself with the black, sketchy trees against the sky and blent with the ragged barbs of smoke that depended from cottage chimneys. The wind had been boisterous enough, and would have torn it away on a cantering jaunt not many minutes ago, but, surcharged as it was now with blinding snow, it had its own liberty to look after, and paid little heed to anything else.

The snow came on thicker and thicker, and had begun to whiten the streets by the time David reached Mr. Griffin's house, and now, as he stood shocked and bewildered in the garden again, it lay deep and dreadfully silent as far as the eye could reach. Had he heard truly? Had he, for the first time in a long, and honest, and reputable life, been called a thief? And by the man whom his heart had overflowed in gratitude to but a moment before! David Dubbs a thief! And what of? What had he stolen? Oh, it was cruel to his poor old heart! "And the girls so merry, even now," he thought. How; how could he go to them with these bitter tidings? To be deprived of even the poor means his pen had faithfully and honestly earned for them; to toil so long, so wearily for the meed of a thief, for the name of a thief! and he wept in his utter woe.

His hat was still on his head, his coat was undone, his scarf had fallen back on his shoulders; his poor old eyes were wide apart again, now, and the wind tugged at his scanty hair, and the snow, no whiter than itself, sifted through it and drifted into the folds of his clothes. But, stunned, and tortured, and despairing though he was, the old clerk staggered on insensibly homeward. Back through the dreary trees; back through the drifted streets; back to the bridge, where he stopped by some fatal impulse and leaned near a bleak abutment that overlooked the river—gazing, gazing, gazing in a blank stare at the driving channel below. The thought, the lurking purpose was shadowed dimly on his distraught mind. The cold, rolling river once passed, the seething cakes of ice once passed, and it would soon be over, soon be over. Life had been a worthless gift to him. His youth had been falsely colored by the visions of childhood; his age had been falsely colored by the ambitions of youth. Nothing he had looked to in the distance ever had grown into reality. Why should he survive his good name! And he clutched the stones and raised himself up and quivered at the top of the stone wall.

But now his hand relaxed, and his face, clouded and suffering before, fell into a calmer look of attention, almost a smile broke over it, and he gazed out against the sky as if transfixed.

It was the vision that had, like the pillar of cloud by day and of fire by night, preceded and gladdened him on his way; the scene of his happy, unsuspecting girls; of the pale Little Scout—whose simple touch would then have instantly revived and soothed him, whose tender love was his comfort, his sanctuary from pursuing evils; the scene of his old home, far cosier, far more beloved, far more cheerful for all its homeliness, for all its poverty, than the more pretentious one of Emanuel Griffin; the scene of lowly pleasures it had cherished; of the bitter trials it had assuaged; and, finally, of the bright, laughing group he had left there, oh! so little prepared, so little conscious of the blight he would bring among them. This vision, these thoughts had flowed in upon his already disturbed mind, and had driven quite away all consciousness of where he was or how long he had stood in the bitter cold, when a policeman—overcoated, and furred, and frozen-bearded,—came by, and, suspecting things to be not altogether right, caught David by the sleeve, and adjusted his scarf and hat, saying,—

"No loafing on the bridge, old man. Move on; move on, now!" at which David started, looked all around him, and then moved on as commanded. His back, always bent, and his gait, always decrepit and shuffling, were now pitiably so, and he had a long, long journey before him; but, thanks be to Him whose omnipotent care protects and watches over the poor in spirit, he had escaped a far longer one. On and on he went, not cold now, not thinking, not in haste; passing thick-coated travellers who ran, and clapped their hands, and swung their arms for warmth; passing gay companies in cabs that rolled over the snow as softly as footsteps on velvet. But he heeded nothing of all this, and staggered onward to his own poor home.

A light was streaming out from the windows of the old warehouse, crossing the snow piled on the platform above and slanting on the heaps beneath. It was an inviting glimmer, a herald from within to all cold travellers without of the blessedness of home, and, as David approached the corner of the court, his eye was greeted cheerily by its "Welcome home!" and, indeed, it was the first thing he had distinctly seen since leaving the house of Mr. Griffin. But his heart failed him. How could he face his dear girls again and tell them of the destitution of to-morrow? Of the worse than poverty? Thus he thought, and lingered, and slunk away by turns, but the ray of home-born light allured him, impassively, into its midst, and as he stood over against the house, a poor, weak, old man, rambling in his mind, and heroically deciding rather to leave them in peace to-night, one more night, and return to them to-morrow, a window was thrown up, and Jacob Tripple, putting forth his head, looked up and down the court, and then directly in front of him, where David stood immovable in the light.

"Why, there he is, now!" he cried. "What's gone amiss, David? What's kept you so long? Here he is! Here he is!" he exclaimed again and again, and, drawing in his head in much less time than the words could be said, Jacob Tripple, followed by the girls, was down-stairs, was—still followed by the girls—out in the snow, and had forcibly carried David up with them.

They laid him on the settee, moaning and crying aloud against Emanuel Griffin, and repeating again and again that they were "Beggars, beggars, beggars!" and exclaiming, "My poor Little Scout! My poor girls! My poor——"

"They shall not suffer, father!" said a new voice, the sound of which raised him up with wide-opened eyes and palsied hands at his head, and a long stare at the speaker—"It's Tom, father. Don't you know me?" repeated the voice.

Know him! How should he know him? tall, and brawny, and whiskered, with pleasant blue eyes, and ruddy cheeks, and good nature streaming from his whole face! Him who, so many years ago,—a beardless youth—had run off to California after gold bubbles, and whom little good had been heard of when anything at all was heard of him. Know him? Of course he did not; but, as he sat down beside him on the settee and shook his old hand, David put his arms about his neck, and hung his head upon his bosom, and saw, in imagination, the thriftless boy of long ago whom he loved for all his waywardness.

Tom's strong arms soon bore him to his old seat near the fire, and, for the first time, David's wandering eye noticed the bower of green holly and red-berried mistletoe that decked the room. General Washington was loaded with it. The old clock, actually striking in a cheerier voice the hour of nine, had its full share. The dresser hid in festoons of it. Even David's chair had its sprig. But what was that on the floor? An opened trunk, like a cloven pomegranate, displaying within rich trinkets that many a lady might covet?

"Wha—what's it all mean, girls? Tell me, Little Scout," said David, catching her hand. "What happened to me? I thought I came home—home to tell you Griffin threw me out in the snow, and called me a thief, and how all of them scowled and cried out at me, and I thought——" then, looking at the tall man, he cried again,—

"Tom, is it so? Is it so, my dear boy?"

"Yes, father," said Tom, slowly, to calm him, "it is, happily, all so."

Then his little daughter, who had stood by his side through it all, kissed him, and said,—

"Come, father, look at the pretty presents Tom has brought us and you. See here's a beautiful new coat hanging on your peg for you, and Molly and Polly are as gay as any ladies," and she led him, tottering and feeble, to the loaded table—no longer ashamed of its defaced back beneath the pile of gifts it bore.

Then Mr. Tripple, hand in hand with the unresisting Polly, and Molly, and Tom, an unbroken circuit of cheery faces that electrified David Dubbs into a wrinkled smile in spite of lingering grief, clustered around the table and exclaimed aloud with admiration at the gifts Tom had brought.

But David, still overshadowed by the events of the afternoon, said, in a quivering voice,—

"But to-morrow, children, to-morrow! I am discharged by Griffin; we shall starve to-morrow!"

"Not while I'm about," laughed Tom. "Come, come, be calm, and I'll tell you all about it."

And he did tell of the long years of hope and distress, of despair when unconsciously within reach of fortune; of its final realization and of its golden yield. "So here I am, father, and your old hand shall write no more for Emanuel Griffin."

Then said Dolly, "You don't speak, father; you are surely not sorry?"

Sorry! He was stifled with gratitude; he was transforming into his old self. The familiar tenderness of her voice opened the floodgates of his heart, and he burst into a louder "Hurrah" than over Griffin's turkey, and kissed them all around, Mr. Tripple included, and, indeed, the day had been so successfully employed on the part of that gentleman that his early entrance into the family was far from problematical—so of course David did perfectly right.

Polly here broke in, "And, father, it was Tom who brought the note, and Tom who planned the surprise for you. What did it say, Tom? you can tell us now."

He laughed quietly, and then said, as if he were reading impressively from the open sheet to Mr. Griffin himself, and making him writhe under his coolness,—

"Emanuel Griffin,

"Sir: The connection of my father, David Dubbs, Esq., with your counting-house, will cease from this day forth.

"Sir, your obedient servant,
"Thomas Dubbs."

Told by an English Tourist.

"He seemed to be a kind of connecting link between the old times and the new, and to be, withal, a little antiquated in the taste of his accomplishments."

Irving.

A STILL CHRISTMAS.

It was Christmas eve in the year of our Lord 1653. The snow, which had fallen fitfully throughout the day, shrouded in white the sloping roofs and narrow London streets, and lay in little, sparkling heaps on every jutting cornice or narrow window-ledge where it could find a resting-place. But in the west the setting sun shone clearly, firing the steeples into sudden glory and gilding every tiny pane of glass that faced its dying splendor. The thoroughfares were strangely silent and deserted. The roving groups that had been wont at this season to fill them with boisterous merriment, the noise, the bustle, the good cheer of Christmas—all were lacking. No maskers roamed from street to street, jingling their bells, beating their mighty drums, and bidding the delighted crowd to make way for the Lord of Misrule. No shouts of "Noel! Noel!" rang through the frosty air. No children gathered round their neighbors' doors, singing quaint carols and forgotten glees, and bearing off rich guerdon in the shape of apples, nuts, and substantial Christmas buns. In place of the old-time gayety a dreary silence reigned through the deserted highways, and down the narrow footwalk, with even step and half-shut eyes, tramped the Puritan herald, ringing his bell and proclaiming ever and anon in measured tones, "No Christmas! No Christmas!"

In sober and sad-hued garments was the herald arrayed, with leathern boots that defied the snow and a copious mantle enveloping his sturdy frame. Now and then he stopped to warn a couple of belated idlers that they would do well to separate and go quietly to their homes. Now and then a little child peeped at him timorously from a doorway, and, overawed by his sombre aspect and heavy frown, retreated rapidly to hide its fears in the safe shelter of its mother's gown. Men shook their heads as he went by, and muttered something that was not always complimentary to his presence; and women shrugged their shoulders and sighed, and thought, perchance, of other Christmases in the past, with Yule-logs burning on the hearth and stray kisses snatched beneath the mistletoe. From a latticed window a girl's face peered at him with such a light of laughing malice in the brown eyes that the Puritan, catching sight of their wicked gleam, paused a moment, as though to reprove the maiden for her forwardness, or to inquire what mischief was afoot under this humble roof. But the night was growing chill, and he had still far to go. It might not be worth while to waste words of counsel on one so evidently godless; and, with a heavier scowl than usual, he tramped on, swinging his bell with lusty force. "No Christmas! No Christmas!" echoed through the darkening streets, and, as he passed, the girl contracted her features into a grimace that would have done credit to the wide-mouthed gargoyle of a Gothic cathedral.

"Cicely, Cicely!" cried a voice, at this juncture, from within, "close the shutters, do, and come and help me."

Cicely, who had been inclined to stare out a little longer, shot the heavy oaken bolt into its socket, and, opening a door leading to the inner room, disclosed a scene whose ruddy cheerfulness shone all the brighter in contrast to the dreary streets outside. A mighty bunch of fagots blazed and crackled on the hearth, and above the carved chimney-place hung branches of holly, their scarlet, berries glowing deeply in the firelight. In one corner, half-veiled by a tapestry curtain, a waxen Bambino nestled in its little manger, while before it burned a small copper lamp. Wreaths of holly and ivy bedecked the doors, and, standing tip-toed on a tall wooden chair, a young girl was even now striving to fasten these securely with the aid of a very old and wrinkled woman, who seemed more competent to admire than to assist the undertaking.

"Some bigger berries, pray, Catherine," she said, impatiently; "and, Cicely, if you feel you have loitered enough, hand me those two long ivy branches. They should droop gracefully—so! And now stand off a little way and tell me how it looks."

The younger sister obeyed, and, stationing herself in the middle of the room, surveyed the whole effect with much approval. Annis, her fair face flushed with the exertion, balanced herself on her lofty perch and gazed complacently upon her handiwork; while even Mistress Vane, who had been seated quietly on a deep chair by the fireplace, roused herself as from a reverie, and looked half-wistfully around the cheerful room. "What bell was that I heard just now?" she asked.

"The herald's, proclaiming a still Christmas," answered Cicely, promptly; "and he watched me as sourly as though he knew that we were plotting treason."

"Cecil, Cecil!" remonstrated her mother, in alarm. "Surely you did nothing imprudent."

"I?" returned Cicely, apparently oblivious as to what she had done. "I cast up the whites of my eyes, as though repeating psalms for mine own inward sustainment; and seeing me so piously disposed, he was fain to pass on to the correction of greater sinners."

"That were well-nigh impossible," said her sister, laughing; but Mistress Vane only looked anxious and disturbed. The sense of insecurity to which Annis was indifferent, and which Cicely at fourteen found absolutely amusing, weighed heavily on the older woman, who had a better understanding of the danger, and who had suffered cruelly in the past. Husband and son had fallen for a lost cause, confiscation had devoured the larger portion of her once fair inheritance; and now, with her two young daughters, she found herself beset by perils, harassed by stringent laws, and at the mercy of any ill-wind fate might blow her. Cromwell's mighty arm held the fretful country in subjection, making the name of England great and terrible abroad, and silencing every whisper of disaffection at home. The Puritans, in their hour of triumph, stamped upon the land the impress of their strong and bitter individuality; and a morose asceticism, part real and part affected, crushed out of life all the innocent pleasure of living. With every man determined to be better than his neighbor, the competition in saintliness ran high. Under its vigorous stimulus the May-pole and the Yule-log were alike branded as heathenish observances, the Christmas-pie became a "pye of abomination," and all amusements, from the drama to bear-baiting, were censured with impartial severity. Feast-days were abolished, and even to display the emblems of the Nativity was held to be sedition. The Established Church, cowed and shorn of its splendor, was treated with surly contempt; the Catholics were altogether beyond the pale of charity. It was not a time calculated to promote festivity; yet, while the heralds proclaimed through the frosty streets that Christmas at last was dead, Annis Vane, with holly and ivy, with Yule-dough and Babie-cake, was making all things ready for its mysterious birth. And as she worked she sang softly under breath the refrain of a carol she had learned at her nurse's knee,—

"This endris night
I saw a sight,
A star as bright as day;
And ever among
A maiden sung
Lullay, by-by, lullay."

"Is it not strange, mother," she said, breaking suddenly off, "that men should deem it a mark of holiness to cast derision on the birth-night of their Saviour?"

"Let us be just even to our enemies," replied Mistress Vane, gently. "They think not to deride the Nativity, so much as to condemn the riotous fashion in which Christians were wont to keep the feast. There have been times, Annis, when the Lord of Misrule did more discredit to this holy season than does the Puritan to-day."

Annis opened her blue eyes to their very utmost. This view of the matter was one she was hardly prepared to accept. "Why, dearest mother," she protested, "when should we venture to be happy, if not on Christmas-day? And how can we show ourselves too joyful for our salvation? And did not his most blessed majesty King

Charles knight with his own royal hand a Lord of Misrule who held court in the Middle Temple?"

Mistress Vane smiled at her daughter's vehemence. She knew more about these jovial monarchs and their courts than Annis did, and it may even be that his most blessed majesty's approval carried less weight to her experienced mind. But in these dark and chilly days a little enthusiasm was helpful in keeping one's heart warm, and she was far too wise a mother to disparage it. "Truly they made a brave show then upon Christmas-day," she admitted, "for the lord mayor and his corporation, a goodly company of gentlemen, rode in procession to the church of St. Thomas Acon, and thence to dine together with many pleasant ceremonies. And stoups of wine and huge venison pasties were despatched to the Temple for the stay and comfort of the mock-court, who made merry all day long. And the streets were crowded, far into the night, with maskers and revellers; and even the poor might for once forget their poverty, and were welcome to the brawn and plum-broth of their richer neighbors."

"And now we have nothing of all this!" cried Cicely, with passionate regret. "Nothing to look at and nothing to hear save the cracked bell of a dingy herald, who does not even ride a hobby-horse like the merry heralds of old. In truth, Master Prynne hath made good his own words when he holds that Christmas should be rather a day of mourning than one of rejoicing."

"Not so thought my godfather, kind Master Breton," said Annis, thoughtfully. "For he hath written that it is the duty of Christians to rejoice for the remembrance of Christ and for the maintenance of good-fellowship. 'I hold it,' he hath said, 'a memory of the Heaven's love and the world's peace, the mirth of the honest and the meeting of the friendly.'"

Cicely's eyes danced with glee. "That were well remembered," she said, mockingly; "if, now, you can but tell us in turn what your godfather's nephew, Captain Rupert Breton, hath thought upon the matter."

Annis flushed scarlet, and the quick tears welled into her eyes as she turned them reproachfully upon her sister. It was not easy for her to think of her absent lover and maintain the cheerful frame of mind she deemed appropriate to the season. The shores of France seemed very far away that night, and the long months that had elapsed since the defeat at Worcester stretched backward like a lifetime, as she recalled his last hurried farewell. He had ridden hard and risked much for those few words, and patiently and bravely she had waited ever since, hoping, praying, turning her face steadily to the brighter side, and keeping ever in mind the happy hour which should reunite them to each other. Now, in silence, she bound together the last green boughs and put all in order for the night. Old Catherine had long since gone off, yawning and blinking, to bed, and Cicely, half-asleep, nodded over the dying fire. Only her mother watched her, with eyes of loving scrutiny, and Annis smiled brightly as she kissed the careworn face. "I shall not cry myself to sleep to-night," she said, resolutely. "This is a time for gladness; for the star of Bethlehem is shining in the sky, and the birth of the Lord is at hand."

Bright glowed the Christmas-logs on the capacious hearth till every pointed leaf and scarlet holly-berry shone in the generous firelight.

> "Whosoever against holly doth cry,
> In a rope shall be hung full high."

For, when the oak and ash trees babbled to the wind, and betrayed the Saviour's hiding-place, the holly, the ivy, and the pine kept the secret hidden in their silent hearts; and for this good deed they stand green and living under winter's icy breath, while their companions shiver naked in the blast. Not till the risen sun has danced on Easter morn shall the oak adorn a Christian household and prove itself forgiven. The Christmas-pie—the Christ-cradle, as the Saxons used to call it—had been baked in its oblong dish in memory of the manger at Bethlehem, with the star of the Magi cut deeply in the swelling crust. The Yule-dough, cunningly moulded into the likeness of a little babe, had been carefully laid by as a sovereign protector from the evils of fire, floods, carnage, and—so say some ancient writers—from the bite of rabid dogs. Annis Vane, decked out in the bravest array her altered fortunes would permit, knelt by the blazing hearth. Her ruff was of the finest lace, and a row of milk-white pearls clasped her slender throat. She shaded her face from the fire, and piled up shining cones of bright-brown nuts that seemed to tempt the flames.

The Cavalier From France

"All we lack now is the mistletoe," she said, half-despondently. "It was no easy task to find the holly and bring it home unnoticed; but we cannot gather mistletoe near London, and there is none for sale throughout the city."

"Of what use is the mistletoe," said the practical Cicely, "when we are but three women here alone? We can kiss each other as readily under a sprig of ivy, and we can fire our nuts without the help of man or lad, provided only we keep one in our minds. Of whom shall I think, Annis?" she queried, wrinkling up her pretty forehead in anxious perplexity over so disturbing a doubt.

"You are far too young to think of men at all," answered Annis, reprovingly, and with all the conscious superiority of age. "Nor do you know enough as yet to make such pastime profitable."

Cicely's brows drew together with a frown which plainly indicated the nature of the retort upon her lips, but a glance from her mother checked her. "The word uttered in vexation is better left unspoken," said Mistress Vane, with gentle authority. "And I am waiting here, not to listen to disputes, which in these stormy times have grown wearisome, but to hear the Christmas carol promised me to-night."

Annis, with flushed cheeks, took down from the wall a little mandolin of Spanish workmanship, and, striking a few chords, began the carol, in which Cicely, after sacrificing some moments to ill-temper, concluded presently to join, her clear flute-notes rising high above her sister's weaker tones,—

> "When Christ was born of Mary free,
> In Bethlehem, in that fair citie,
> Angels sungen with mirth and glee,
> In Excelsis Gloria!
> "Herdsmen beheld these angels bright
> To them appeared with great light,
> And said, God's Son is born this night,
> In Excelsis Gloria!
> "The King is comen to save kind,
> Even in Scripture as we find;
> Therefore this song have we in mind,

In Excelsis Gloria!
"Then, dear Lord, for thy great grace,
Grant us in bliss to see thy face,
Where we may sing to thee solace,
In Excelsis Gloria!"

As the sounds died into silence there stood one in the icy streets and listened. No self-elected saint was he, scenting out treason to the Commonwealth, but a cavalier from France, with his love-locks shorn for sweet prudence's sake, and a mighty mantle enveloping him from head to foot. If Annis Vane had waited, and hoped, and built up her faith in the cheer of Christmas-night, the joy she coveted was very near at last. After lingering a few moments, as though on the chance of hearing more, the stranger advanced and knocked sharply at the heavily-barred door. It was opened in due season and with great caution by old Catherine, who evidently thought the hour ill-chosen for a newcomer, and mistrusted sorely the purpose of his visit. He allowed her scant time, however, to threaten or expostulate, but, putting her gently on one side, stepped to the inner room. There, pale with anxiety and terror, Mistress Vane leaned forward in her chair, while Cicely, half-frightened, half-defiant, grasped her mother's skirt. Before the fire stood Annis, her blue eyes shining like stars, a round, red spot burning feverishly in each cheek, her lace ruff rising and falling distressfully with the heaving bosom within. The mandolin had fallen from her hands; the ruddy firelight lit up her slight figure and fair, disordered curls. She stood thus for a moment, swaying breathless betwixt hope and fear, then, with a low, joyous cry, sprang forward into her lover's arms.

Welcome now the good cheer of Christmas-night! Welcome the Christmas-pie, the pasty of venison, the pudding stuffed with plums, and the flagon of old wine. Love is a brave appetizer when backed by long fasting and a ten hours' ride, and Captain Breton brought all the vigor of youth and happiness and of a noble hunger to bear upon the viands. The glow of the cheerful room was infinitely comforting to the tired traveller; the sight of Annis's happy face put fresh hope and courage in his heart. He had much to tell of the gay court of France, and of the royal exile, who should one day, God willing, sit on his father's throne. Nor were there lacking adventures and dangers of his own to give flavor to the narrative, nor plans for the future, colored with all the happy confidence of youth. He had come home to win his bride, and to carry her away to brighter scenes until this soured and gloomy England should be merrie England once more. "He who would keep a light heart within London walls," said he, "must needs be very sure of heaven, as are Master Prynne and Master Philip Stubbes, or very much in love, as am I. It lacks but a covered cart and a bell in every street to make one feel the Black Death is upon us. If you can laugh in such an atmosphere of melancholy, Annis, what will you do in France?"

"Mayhap if I laugh enough in sober London I shall grow too giddy and forward in foolish France," returned Annis, gayly; "unless——"

"Unless what, dear heart?"

"Unless while I am safe in Paris you are fighting the battles of the king in England. Then tears will come easier than laughter, as in truth they have done of late."

"Wherever I may be, your prayers will prove my bulwark," said Captain Breton, confidently. "It would take more than a silver bullet to find its way to my heart while you are besieging heaven's doors in the tumultuous fashion that only women can attain. I bear a charmed life as long as you remember your petitions."

Annis answered with a look, and Cicely, nestling by her mother's chair, watched her sister with wide, serious eyes. To the child standing on the threshold of womanhood the presence of love carries with it an intoxicating flavor of mystery. It is something that fills her alike with envy and a vague resentment, with wonder and an indefinable desire. Its commonest expression is a perverse antipathy to one of the lovers, with an irrational increase of affection for the other; and in this case Captain Breton came in for his full share of Cicely's smothered anger and disdain. He, meanwhile, in happy unconsciousness, chancing to meet the brown eyes lifted dreamily to his own, and noting the upward curve of the short, sweet lip, thought within himself that this elfish little Cicely was growing almost as pretty as her sister—a judgment which proves conclusively the blindness of love; for Annis, though fair and comely to look upon, came no nearer to her young sister's beauty than does the pink-tipped daisy to the half-opened rosebud uncurling slowly in the sun. At present, the girl, seeing that she was watched, turned away her head pettishly and eyed the leaping flames.

"Annis said to-night there was but one thing lacking to her Christmas cheer," she remarked, after a pause, and with the too evident intention of saying something vexatious.

"And that was I!" interposed the cavalier, with the ready assurance of a lover.

"It was not you at all," returned Cicely, "but the mistletoe. We gathered the other greens ourselves, but there was no mistletoe to be found within or without the gates of London."

"By a happy chance we can proceed as though we had it," said Captain Breton, contentedly, while Annis crimsoned like a rose. "It is a welcome little plant, and carries a merry message; but if it be banished in these saintly days, we obstinate sinners must kiss without its sanction."

"But the maid who is not kissed on Christmas-night beneath the mistletoe will never be a wife during the coming year," persisted Cicely, who had laid down her line of attack and was not to be driven therefrom.

"Now, will you wager your ring or your new ear-drop on that, little sister?" said the captain, laughing at the threat. "Or have you a trinket that you value less to risk in such a cause?"

Cicely, deeply affronted, puckered up her brow and drew closer to her mother; but Annis, far too happy to be vexed, leaned over and kissed the pouting lips. With her, joy meant thanksgiving, and her heart was singing—singing the song of the angel of Judea: "In Excelsis Gloria!"

A Norseman's Saga.

"As he sat there with a sou'wester down over his ears, in a long pilot coat, his figure appeared to assume quite supernatural proportions, and you might almost imagine that you had one of the old Vikings before you."

Asbjörnsen.

THROND.

There was once a man named Alf, who had raised great expectations among his fellow-parishioners because he excelled most of them both in the work he accomplished and in the advice he gave. Now, when this man was thirty years old, he went to live up the mountain, and cleared a piece of land for farming, about fourteen miles from any settlement. Many people wondered how he could endure thus depending on himself for companionship, but they were still more astonished when, a few years later, a young girl from the valley, and one, too, who had been the gayest of the gay at all the social gatherings and dances of the parish, was willing to share his solitude.

This couple were called "the people in the wood," and the man was known by the name of "Alf in the wood." People viewed him with inquisitive eyes when they met him at church or at work, because they did not understand him; but neither did he take the trouble to give them any explanation of his conduct. His wife was only seen in the parish twice, and on one of these occasions it was to present a child for baptism.

This child was a son, and he was called Thrond. When he grew larger his parents often talked about needing help, and, as they could not afford to take a full-grown servant, they hired what they called "a half:" they brought into their house a girl of fourteen, who took care of the boy while the father and mother were busy in the field.

This girl was not the brightest person in the world, and the boy soon observed that his mother's words were easy to comprehend, but that it was hard to get at the meaning of what Ragnhild said. He never talked much with his father, and he was rather afraid of him, for the house had to be kept very quiet when he was home. One Christmas Eve—they were burning two candles on the table, and the father was drinking from a white flask—the father took the boy up in his arms and set him on his lap, looked him sternly in the eyes, and exclaimed,—

"Ugh, boy!" Then he added more gently,—"Why, you are not so much afraid. Would you have the courage to listen to a story?"

The boy made no reply, but he looked full in his father's face. His father then told him about a man from Vaage, whose name was Blessom. This man was in Copenhagen for the purpose of getting the king's verdict in a law-suit he was engaged in, and he was detained so long that Christmas eve overtook him there. Blessom was greatly annoyed at this, and, as he was sauntering about the streets fancying himself at home, he saw a very large man, in a white, short coat, walking in front of him.

"How fast you are walking!" said Blessom.

"I have a long distance to go in order to get home this evening," replied the man.

"Where are you going?"

"To Vaage," answered the man, and walked on.

"Why, that is very nice," said Blessom, "for that is where I am going, too."

"Well, then, you may ride with me, if you will stand on the runners of my sledge," answered the man, and turned into a side street where his horse was standing.

He mounted his seat and looked over his shoulder at Blessom, who was just getting on the runners.

"You had better hold fast," said the stranger.

Blessom did as he was told, and it was well he did, for their journey was evidently not by land.

"It seems to me that you are driving on the water," cried Blessom.

"I am," said the man, and the spray whirled about them.

But after a while it seemed to Blessom their course no longer lay on the water.

"It seems to me we are moving through the air," said he.

"Yes, so we are," replied the stranger.

But when they had gone still farther, Blessom thought he recognized the parish they were driving through.

"Is not this Vaage?" cried he.

"Yes, now we are there," replied the stranger, and it seemed to Blessom that they had gone pretty fast.

"Thank you for the good ride," said he.

"Thanks to yourself," replied the man, and added, as he whipped up his horse, "Now you had better not look after me."

"No, indeed," thought Blossom, and started over the hills for home.

But just then so loud and terrible a crash was heard behind him that it seemed as if the whole mountain must be tumbling down, and a bright light was shed over the surrounding landscape; he looked round and beheld the stranger in the white coat driving through the crackling flames into the open mountain, which was yawning wide to receive him, like some huge gate. Blossom felt somewhat strange in regard to his travelling companion; and thought he would look in another direction; but as he had turned his head so it remained, and never more could Blossom get it straight again.

The boy had never heard anything to equal this in all his life. He dared not ask his father for more, but early the next morning he asked his mother if she knew any stories. Yes, of course she did; but hers were chiefly about princesses who were in captivity for seven years, until the right prince came along. The boy believed that everything he heard or read about took place close around him.

He was about eight years old when the first stranger entered their door one winter evening. He had black hair, and this was something Thrond had never seen before. The stranger saluted them with a short "Good-evening!" and came forward. Thrond grew frightened and sat down on a cricket by the hearth. The mother asked the man to take a seat on the bench along the wall; he did so, and then the mother could examine his face more closely.

"Dear me! is not this Knud the fiddler?" cried she.

"Yes, to be sure it is. It has been a long time since I played at your wedding."

"Oh, yes; it is quite a while now. Have you been on a long journey?"

"I have been playing for Christmas on the other side of the mountain. But half-way down the slope I began to feel very badly, and I was obliged to come in here to rest."

The mother brought forward food for him; he sat down to the table, but did not say "in the name of Jesus," as the boy had been accustomed to hear. When he had finished eating, he got up from the table, and said,—

"Now I feel very comfortable; let me rest a little while."

And he was allowed to rest on Thrond's bed.

For Thrond a bed was made on the floor. As the boy lay there, he felt cold on the side that was turned away from the fire, and that was the left side. He discovered that it was because this side was exposed to the chill night air; for he was lying out in the wood. How came he in the wood? He got up and looked about him, and saw that there was fire burning a long distance off, and that he was actually alone in the wood. He longed to go home to the fire;

but could not stir from the spot. Then a great fear overcame him; for wild beasts might be roaming about, trolls and ghosts might appear to him; he must get home to the fire; but he could not stir from the spot. Then his terror grew, he strove with all his might to gain self-control, and was at last able to cry, "Mother," and then he awoke.

"Dear child, you have had bad dreams," said she, and took him up.

A shudder ran through him, and he glanced round. The stranger was gone, and he dared not inquire after him.

His mother appeared in her black dress, and started for the parish. She came home with two new strangers, who also had black hair and who wore flat caps. They did not say "in the name of Jesus," when they ate, and they talked in low tones with the father. Afterwards the latter and they went into the barn, and came out again with a large box, which the men carried between them. They placed it on a sled, and said farewell. Then the mother said,—

"Wait a little, and take with you the smaller box he brought here with him."

And she went in to get it. But one of the men said,—

"*He* can have that," and he pointed at Thrond.

"Use it as well as *he* who is now lying here," added the other stranger, pointing at the large box.

Then they both laughed and went on. Thrond looked at the little box which thus came into his possession.

"What is there in it?" asked he.

"Carry it in and find out," said the mother.

He did as he was told, but his mother helped him open it. Then a great joy lighted up his face, for he saw something very light and fine lying there.

"Take it up," said his mother.

He put just one finger down on it, but quickly drew it back again in great alarm.

"It cries," said he.

"Have courage," said his mother, and he grasped it with his whole hand and drew it forth from the box.

He weighed it and turned it round, he laughed and felt of it.

"Dear me! what is it?" asked he, for it was as light as a toy.

"It is a fiddle."

This was the way that Thrond Alfson got his first violin.

The father could play a little, and he taught the boy how to handle the instrument; the mother could sing the tunes she remembered from her dancing days, and these the boy learned, but soon began to make new ones for himself. He played all the time he was not at his books; he played until his father once told him he was fading away before his eyes. All the boy had read and heard until that time was put into the fiddle. The tender, delicate string was his mother; the one that lay close beside it, and always accompanied his mother, was Ragnhild. The coarse string, which he seldom ventured to play on, was his father. But of the last solemn string he was half afraid, and he gave no name to it. When he played a wrong note on the E string, it was the cat; but when he took a wrong note on his father's string, it was the ox. The bow was Blessom, who drove from Copenhagen to Vaage in one night. And every tune he played represented something. The one containing the long solemn tones was his mother in her black dress. The one that jerked and skipped was like Moses, who stuttered and smote the rock with his staff. The one that had to be played quietly, with the bow moving lightly over the strings, was the hulder in yonder fog, calling together her cattle, where no one but herself could see.

But the music wafted him onward over the mountains, and a great yearning took possession of his soul. One day, when his father told about a little boy who had been playing at the fair and who had earned a great deal of money, Thrond waited for his mother in the kitchen and asked her softly if he could not go to the fair and play for people.

"Whoever heard of such a thing!" said his mother; but she immediately spoke to his father about it.

"He will get out into the world soon enough," answered the father; and he spoke in such a way that the mother did not ask again.

Shortly after this, the father and mother were talking at table about some new settlers who had recently moved up on the mountain and were about to be married. They had no fiddler for the wedding, the father said.

"Could not I be the fiddler?" whispered the boy, when he was alone in the kitchen once more with his mother.

"What, a little boy like you?" said she; but she went out to the barn where his father was and told him about it.

"He has never been in the parish," she added; "he has never seen a church."

"I should not think you would ask about such things," said Alf; but neither did he say anything more, and so the mother thought she had permission. Consequently she went over to the new settlers and offered the boy's services.

"The way he plays," said she, "no little boy has ever played before;" and the boy was to be allowed to come.

What joy there was at home! Thrond played from morning until evening and practised new tunes; at night he dreamed about them: they bore him far over the hills, away to foreign lands, as though he were afloat on sailing clouds. His mother made a new suit of clothes for him; but his father would not take part in what was going on.

The last night he did not sleep, but thought out a new tune about the church which he had never seen. He was up early in the morning, and so was his mother, in order to get him his breakfast, but he could not eat. He put on his new clothes and took his fiddle in his hand, and it seemed to him as though a bright light were glowing before his eyes. His mother accompanied him out on the flag-stone, and stood watching him as he ascended the slopes; it was the first time he had left home.

His father got quietly out of bed, and walked to the window; he stood there, following the boy with his eyes until he heard the mother out on the flag-stone, then he went back to bed and was lying down when she came in.

She kept stirring about him, as if she wanted to relieve her mind of something. And finally it came out,—

"I really think I must walk down to the church and see how things are going."

He made no reply, and therefore she considered the matter settled, dressed herself, and started.

It was a glorious, sunny day, the boy walked rapidly onward, he listened to the song of the birds and saw the sun glittering among the foliage, while he proceeded on his way, with his fiddle under his arm. And when he reached the bride's house, he was still so occupied with his own thoughts, that he observed neither the bridal splendor nor the procession; he merely asked if they were about to start, and learned that they were. He walked on in advance with his fiddle, and he played the whole morning into it, and the tones he produced resounded through the trees.

"Will we soon see the church?" he asked over his shoulder.

For a long time he received only "No" for an answer, but at last some one said,—

"As soon as you reach that crag yonder, you will see it."

He threw his newest tune into the fiddle, the bow danced on the strings, and he kept his eyes fixed intently before him. There lay the parish right in front of him!

The first thing he saw was a little light mist, curling like smoke on the opposite mountain side. His eyes wandered over the green meadow and the large houses, with windows which glistened beneath the scorching rays of the sun, like the glacier on a winter's day. The houses kept increasing in size, the windows in number, and here on one side of him lay the enormous red house, in front of which horses were tied; little children were playing on a hill, dogs were sitting watching them. But everywhere there penetrated a long, heavy tone, that shook him from head to foot, and everything he saw seemed to vibrate with that tone. Then suddenly he saw a large, straight house, with a tall, glittering staff reaching up to the skies. And below, a hundred windows blazed, so that the house seemed to be enveloped in flames. This must be the church, the boy thought, and the music must come from it! Round about stood a vast multitude of people, and they all looked alike! He put them forthwith into relations with the church, and thus acquired a respect mingled with awe for the smallest child he saw.

"Now I must play," thought Thrond, and tried to do so.

But what was this? The fiddle had no longer any sound in it. There must be some defect in the strings; he examined, but could find none.

"Then it must be because I do not press on hard enough," and he drew his bow with a firmer hand; but the fiddle seemed as if it were cracked.

He changed the tune that was meant to represent the church into another, but with equally bad results; no music was produced, only squeaking and wailing. He felt the cold sweat start out over his face; he thought of all these wise people who were standing here and perhaps laughing him to scorn, this boy who at home could play so beautifully, but who here failed to bring out a single tone!

"Thank God that mother is not here to see my shame!" said he softly to himself, as he played among the people; but lo! there she stood, in her black dress, and she shrank farther and farther away.

At that moment he beheld far up on the spire the black-haired man who had given him the fiddle. "Give it back to me," he now shouted, laughing, and stretching out his arms, and the spire went up and down with him, up and down. But the boy took the fiddle under one arm, screaming, "You shall not have it!" and, turning, ran away from the people, beyond the houses, onward through meadow and field, until his strength forsook him, and then sank to the ground.

There he lay for a long time, with his face toward the earth, and when finally he looked round he saw and heard only God's infinite blue sky that floated above him, with its everlasting sough. This was so terrible to him that he had to turn his face to the ground again. When he raised his head once more his eyes fell on his fiddle, which lay at his side.

"This is all your fault!" shouted the boy, and seized the instrument with the intention of dashing it to pieces, but hesitated as he looked at it.

"We have had many a happy hour together," said he, then paused. Presently he said, "The strings must be severed, for they are worthless." And he took out a knife and cut. "Oh!" cried the E string, in a short, pained tone. The boy cut. "Oh!" wailed the next, but the boy cut. "Oh!" said the third, mournfully; and he paused at the fourth. A sharp pain seized him; that fourth string, to which he never dared give a name, he did not cut. Now a feeling came over him that it was not the fault of the strings that he was unable to play, and just then he saw his mother walking slowly up the slope toward where he was lying, that she might take him home with her. A greater fright than ever overcame him; he held the fiddle by the severed strings, sprang to his feet, and shouted down to her,—

"No, mother! I will not go home again until I can play what I have seen to-day."

Contributed by An Oriental Traveller.

"A great, long devil of a Spahi in his red burnous."

Daudet.

CHRISTMAS IN THE DESERT.

I.

It seemed all too good to be true: the rest from labor, the swift flight across southern seas, the landing, amid strange, dark faces on a burnished shore, the slow, delicious journey through tamarisk groves and palm forests, and the halt in the Desert that came at last.

I had been doing for the last twelve months what young artists and authors are constantly doing, to their own ruin and the justifiable ill-humor of critics, namely, working against the grain. A sweet, generous, and beautiful Patroness, seeing me on the high road to brain fever or hopeless mediocrity, stepped forward in time, and sent me to the Desert. If ever I achieve anything excellent, it will be owing to that lady, the Vittoria Colonna of her humble Michael Angelo. My little sister Mary came with me, and, when I tell you that she was a teacher in a school, you will easily understand what an intoxicating thing it was for her to see a new world every day, and have nothing to do frommorning, till night. The poor child could hardly believe in an existence without Czerny's scales being played on three or four pianos at once, and a barrel organ and brass band in the street. "Oh, Tom!" she would say to me, a dozen times a day, "I've got C scale and 'Wait for the Wagon' on my brain, and can't get rid of them;" so that I verily believe to my beautiful Vittoria Colonna Mary's present well-being is due as much as my own.

We halted at a little military station on the borders of the Great Sahara, about a week before Christmas-day. The weather was perfect, and not too warm. A delicious, mellow atmosphere enveloped palm, and plain, and mosque; the air, blown across thousands and thousands of acres of wild thyme and rosemary, refreshed us like wine: we seemed to have new souls and new bodies given us, and were as free from care as the swallows flying overhead. Travellers never came to Teschoun, as this little oasis is called; but we had placed ourselves under the guidance of an enterprising Frenchman, who transacted all sorts of business on the road between Mascara and Fig-gig, the last French post in the Desert. His name was Dominique, and I shall always look upon him as the most remarkable man I ever knew. He was as witty as Sydney Smith, as clever at expediences as Robinson Crusoe, as shrewd a politician as Machiavelli, as apt at languages as Mezzofanti, and as brave as Garibaldi. Being a bachelor, Dominique was none the less ready to receive us, and, with the help of an old Corsican named Napoleon, made us very comfortable. When Dominique was carrying His Imperial Majesty's mails to some remote stations southward, or had gone to an Arab fair to buy cattle, Napoleon catered for us and cooked for us, and did both admirably. Both master and servant spiced their dishes plentifully with that mother-wit, never seen in such perfection as in crude colonies where people without it would fare so ill.

"What are we to do for society for poor mademoiselle?" asked Dominique, as he served our first dinner. "Monsieur can amuse himself with the officers of the garrison, but there are no ladies here."

"When my brother is out, I shall stay at home and talk to Napoleon," Mary said, with a mock assumption of dignity. "I don't want to be amused, Monsieur Dominique."

"Mon Dieu, mademoiselle! the officers of the garrison will fall in love with you, and that ought to amuse you better than talking to Napoleon," Dominique answered. "It's a very dull life they lead here, these poor officers; and if it weren't for hunting gazelles and hyenas, and playing the deuce with the Arabs, they'd die of ennui; but a pretty young lady like you will turn their heads soon enough."

Mary blushed, and tried to turn the conversation.

"What do they do with themselves all day long?" she asked.

"I'll tell you that quickly enough, mademoiselle. M. le Commandant has to see that the Cadi gets what he can out of the Sheiks, and the Sheiks get what they can out of the tribes, and that the tribes hold their tongue. That is what the Commandant has to do, young lady, and he does it pretty well. M. le Capitaine has an easier time of it, except when there is an insurrection, and then he makes a raid against the Arabs, and after keeping his men out of their way very cleverly, sticks up the French flag somewhere in the Desert and comes home. M. le Lieutenant does odd jobs for the Commandant and the Capitaine, and plays the flute; but we have got M. le Général down here for a few days, and he is setting everybody to work. I dare say the end of it will be an expedition into the Desert. You may look, monsieur. I'm not talking at random, I assure you; generals love war as umbrella-makers love bad weather; and it is easier to make people fight than it is to make it rain."

"I think French officers must be a wicked set; I hope none of them will come near us," Mary said. "The poor Arabs! how my heart bleeds for them."

"Tiens! mademoiselle, there is no reason for your heart to bleed. Big flies live on little ones all the world over; and if the French eat up the Arabs, the Arabs eat up each other. The officers are very nice, harmless gentlemen, I assure you; and as to the Commandant, though he thinks fighting the best fun in the world, he wouldn't hurt a fly. To see him pet his little gazelle would make you cry. She's the only lady in the place, and I believe, if she died, it would break his heart. But people must have something to be fond of. My old Napoleon, yonder, has taken a fancy to a cat, and when the cat dies, Napoleon will be as lost as his namesake the Emperor was at St. Helena. Listen a moment; that's the Lieutenant practising on his flute: he has a little lodging next door."

The Lieutenant played very prettily, and Mary seemed to like his playing much better than Dominique's stories. As her room adjoined the Lieutenant's, she seemed likely to have the full benefit of his musical capacities; but I do not think she lay awake to be serenaded that night. We were fairly intoxicated with the sweet air of the Desert we had been breathing all day, and went to bed at eight o'clock, too tired and happy to dream.

Next morning Dominique informed us that he had himself delivered our letter of introduction to M. le Commandant, who promised to wait upon us in the course of the day. Not knowing at what hour we might expect him, we set to work immediately after breakfast to prepare my room for the reception of so distinguished a visitor. I helped Mary as well as I was able, and, when nothing remained to do but the dusting, retired into a recess to trim my beard.

An Englishwoman is never so well dressed as when she emerges from her bedroom at early morning; and I must say that Mary looked the daintiest little housewife possible to conceive as she went about dusting and polishing in a pink cambric dress and tiny black apron. But, neat as she was, and neat as my beard and the room were in a fair way of becoming, we were overwhelmed with surprise and confusion at what followed, for quite suddenly the door was thrown open; there was a military tramp and a rattling of a sword outside, and Dominique exclaimed, in a voice of thunder, "M. le Commandant!"

Impassible self-possession is a beautiful quality, and while Mary and I stood blushing and aghast, like school children caught at stealing cherries, M. le Commandant had made a courteous speech, welcoming us to Teschoun. Then we all sat down, and M. le Commandant talked to us. He was a sunburnt, soldierly man about fifty-five, with a rough manner but a kind smile, and we felt at home with him in a moment.

"I presume that monsieur wishes to see as much of the country as possible," he said; "and I shall be enchanted to place at monsieur's disposal horses, and my servant and a spahi as guides. But what will mademoiselle do while her brother is away? I must send her my little gazelle to play with her."

"My sister will like to go with me where it is practicable," I said.

The Commandant opened his eyes, and looked at Mary much as one looks upon a pretty little duckling or a year-old baby.

"Monsieur is evidently jesting," he answered. "Mademoiselle would be too fatigued to undertake such journeys."

"I don't think so," Mary said. "I have no fear, monsieur, and I like to be with my brother."

"Ah, what courage you English ladies have! Well, mademoiselle, we will find you a quiet horse, and make everything as pleasant as possible." And after inviting us to dine with him one evening, and bidding us to make use of him in every possible way, he took leave of us.

"How nice he is!" cried Mary, as soon as the door was closed; "if all French officers were like this one, Tom, I think we shall not care how long we stay in the Desert——"

"Your heart has very quickly ceased to bleed for the poor Arabs, I see."

"But how can we be sure that Dominique's stories are all true? No, Tom; I won't believe any harm of this kind-looking Commandant. I only wish he had not come till the room was tidied and I had got on a muslin frock, but, as we are sure of having no more visitors, I'll finish your room and then unpack."

We were fairly at our work again, when another military step sounded, and another sword rattled in the passage outside. This time Dominique's arm swung back the door with less pomposity, and Dominique's voice was a trifle less emphatic as he ushered in "M. le Capitaine."

Again Mary and I scuttled about like young rabbits, and then stood still, staring shyly, and again our embarrassment was met by the calmest nonchalance. The second figure was a man of much more presence than the Commandant. He had the polished, graceful ease of a man of the world, and, though quite as good-natured as the Commandant, his good-nature pleased us less, because it was less spontaneous.

"I hope you will stay some time at Teschoun," he said, looking at Mary. "The ennui of our lives here is terrible. Think of it, mademoiselle; we have no theatre, no music, no society, and no domestic life. To find a lady here is like the miraculous advent of an angel." Mary blushed, and had no courage to make the sprightly answers she had made the Commandant.

The fine air and grand compliments of the Capitaine overcame the little thing, but she looked distractingly pretty as she sat opposite to him, smiling and blushing when he addressed her, and only saying, "Oui, monsieur," or "Non, monsieur," or at most, "Vraiment, monsieur."

"Does mademoiselle ride?" asked the gallant Capitaine.

"Oui, monsieur."

"Then mademoiselle shall ride my little barb; there is hardly such a horse anywhere, mademoiselle, so docile, so sweet-tempered, and so sure-footed. It is not every lady I would trust with my little horse; but I know how an Englishwoman can sit in the saddle, and I am proud to offer it to mademoiselle."

"Je vous remercie bien, monsieur."

Then the Capitaine talked of Christmas-day.

"We will have a little fête-champêtre in mademoiselle's honor," he said; "we will go to the great water-falls of Boisel-Kebir and breakfast there. I will invite my Commandant and all the officers of the garrison. Monsieur can make a sketch and mademoiselle can gather flowers."

We expressed ourselves delighted at the proposal, and, after promising to send Mary ostrich eggs and jackal skins to take to England, the Capitaine left us.

"I don't like the Capitaine as well as the Commandant," Mary said; "but how kind they all are to us! It is as if we were princes on a journey of triumph. Oh, Tom! what days to remember are these!"

"I think your head will be fairly turned, what with the Commandant's dinners and the Capitaine's fêtes-champêtres," I said; "and if the Lieutenant——"

"M. le Lieutenant!" announced Dominique, opening the door calmly, as if nothing was the matter.

We had been twice so shocked and surprised that we had no more embarrassment to expend on the Lieutenant. Indeed, he was rather shy himself, which was the very thing to reassure a warm-hearted, sympathetic little creature like my sister, and they began to talk together without any effort.

He was young and handsome, with a very frank, pleasant expression.

"I am afraid that it is useless for me to offer my poor services," he said, very modestly, "my superior officers having forestalled me; but it will make me very happy to do anything for you. If mademoiselle would like any stuffed birds, or dried flowers and plants, it will give me pleasure to procure them for her; and perhaps monsieur would like me to show him some wonderful things to paint. I draw a little myself, and know where the finest points of view are to be found."

We thanked him heartily, and accepted all that he offered us. As it was now time for our second breakfast, or, more properly speaking, lunch, we pressed him to partake of it with us, which he did. We should not have ventured upon inviting the Commandant, much less the Capitaine, so unceremoniously, but the Lieutenant's diffident manner had set us quite at our ease.

"I have a very humble apartment," he said; "but if monsieur and mademoiselle will visit me, I will do the honors of it with pride and pleasure. I can at least offer them a little music."

"Yes, I know that you play," Mary said, smiling; "our rooms join, and I heard you playing before I went to sleep last night."

"Oh, mademoiselle! I shall never forgive myself if I disturbed you."

"No, indeed, you did not, monsieur. Much as I liked the music, I was too tired to listen to it, and went to sleep all the same."

Then they both laughed gleefully, like children, and the Lieutenant promised to play to her and send her to sleep every night.

After breakfast he accompanied us on a tour of inspection. We soon saw all that there was to see of Teschoun, namely, a little line of bazaars kept by Jews and negroes, a little boulevard of a year's growth, two imposing-looking gates,—one looking towards Morocco, one towards the Sahara,—a straggling camp, and a wall of circumvallation. There were gardens in embryo here and there, but no trees of any size, and not till you had got fairly away from Teschoun could you perceive that its aspect was striking or imposing. Then, looking back from the craggy heights that surrounded it, the white line of the camp and the belt of verdure encircling it like a ribbon, struck the eye as a pleasant contrast to the warm, yellow atmosphere of earth and sky. The warmth and the yellowness were delicious. A fresh, sweet breeze blew across our faces from the Desert. We sat down and drew it in with long, devouring breaths.

A hundred yards behind us, his bright-brown body sharply outlined against the pale, amber-colored sky, stood a little Bedouin smiling down upon us. It was a perfect personification of Eastern life, and I made a sketch, while the Lieutenant told Mary of his hard campaign southward, and his joy at catching the first glimpse of Teschoun from the distance.

When we returned home we found that the Commandant's servant had left a bunch of roses for Mary, with his master's compliments; that the Capitaine's servant had been sent round with his master's horse for her to try, and that the Général had sent word by his aide-de-camp that he would himself have the pleasure of calling upon us that evening.

Mary and I felt utterly overwhelmed by such goodness and condescension. A real starred, laced Général was about to call on us! We could hardly believe that we were our identical, insignificant selves, who, but for you, oh! most sweet and honored Patroness, would have sunk under the burden of toil imposed upon us. But how all was changed! The poor, unknown artist was treated as if he had been Sir Peter Paul Rubens; the humble little school teacher was fêted and flattered like the wife of a conquering commander-in-chief.

We had invited the young Lieutenant to drink tea with us at eight o'clock, and were enjoying a little music after a very sociable fashion, when a noisy excitement seemed to shake the house like a shock of an earthquake, and M. le Général was announced in Dominique's most impressive manner.

M. le Général was by no means an awful-looking person; and, indeed, we had so expended our surprise already, that we had no more at command.

He was an excessively stout, merry person, middle-aged, of a beautiful complexion, and a capacity to wink that would have vulgarized any one else but a general. He made himself very pleasant, accepted a cup of tea, praised Mary's French, said that he intended to dine with us at the Commandant's to-morrow, and told us some laughable stories about the Arabs. I noticed that the Lieutenant seemed quite overawed by the presence of the Général, and sat flute in hand, like a statue. Mary tried to put him at his ease, but to no purpose. It did not mend matters when the Général began first to twit him about his musical accomplishments, and then to catechise him on military matters.

"You were in that affair of '59, in Kabylia, weren't you?" he asked, in that quick, positive, military tone to which we with difficulty get accustomed.

My Little Sister Mary

"Oui, mon Général."

"It was a badly managed thing, I believe. The Kabyles got the better of you more than once, didn't they?"

"I believe so, mon Général."

"Bah!" cried the Général, turning to me. "You see what these young officers know of their trade. I have no doubt that Monsieur le

Lieutenant's musical education is much more advanced, and to serenade mademoiselle suits him much better than to make war against the enemies of his country."

And, at the mention of the enemies of his country, the Général indulged in a wink. When he was ready to go, he sent the Lieutenant to order his horse, much as if he had been a little boy of ten years old; and on taking leave added half a dozen commissions in the same peremptory tone. The poor Lieutenant listened very submissively, but no sooner had the Général dashed down the street, followed by his servant, equally well mounted, than he grew gay and easy again.

As soon as we were alone, Mary brought out her slender supply of gala dresses, and we discussed the important subject of her toilet of the next evening.

"It seems to me," I said, "that if you dress for the Lieutenant, you will displease the Capitaine; if you dress for the Capitaine, you will displease the Commandant; and if you dress for the Commandant, you will displease the Général."

Mary gathered up her fineries in alarm. "Don't you think I had better stay away from the dinner altogether, Tom?"

"By no means," I said; "settle the matter by dressing to please me."

Which she accordingly did, and the result was a semi-moresque, dainty, and glowing bit of costume quite in keeping with the time and place.

II.

Precisely at seven o'clock we presented ourselves at the Commandant's, Mary looking very pretty in her transparent white dress, brilliant sack of Tunis silk, and necklets and bracelets of coral and palm-seeds. The little thing had such loving, dark eyes, such a soft bloom on her cheeks, and such a sweet mouth, that I could hardly blame the Général for wishing to have her sit beside him at dinner. The Commandant, being a little shy, would have given up all his privileges as host, but the Général insisted upon the Commandant leading her in, and she sat between the two. It was very mortifying for the Capitaine and the Lieutenant; the former made an effort to be complimentary and entertaining across the table, but the latter looked quite crestfallen, and hardly raised his eyes from his plate. When we retired to the drawing-room, matters went a little better. The tame gazelle was brought in for Mademoiselle Marie to see; and while the Général and the Commandant had a long discussion on military affairs, the rest of us sported with the pretty creature and made pleasant plans for the morrow. Then an amusing game of cards was set on foot, over which we were growing very merry, when up came the Général and the Commandant.

"Eh, bien!" said the Général, slyly nudging the Capitaine. "We have not been so engrossed, but we heard one or two pleasant things talked of. Upon my word, Capitaine, I am half disposed not to go to Mascara till after your picnic to the water-falls."

"You will do my poor little fête great honor, mon Général," answered the Capitaine, adding, naïvely, "but I think that the wild geese flying northwards means rain."

"Not a bit of it. We shall have no rain until a fortnight after Christmas. Mademoiselle Marie, I shall do myself the honor of offering you one of my horses to ride."

"Mademoiselle has already condescended to accept mine," the Capitaine put in, with stiffness.

"Mademoiselle Marie, this gentleman has no horse fit to carry a lady. The brute he offers you has no more mouth than an elephant. Keep on the safe side and ride mine, which is a lamb, I assure you, mademoiselle,—a lamb."

The Général spoke in jest, but the Capitaine was very near losing his temper. Mary being thus appealed to, thought to extricate herself from the difficulty by declaring herself half afraid to ride either horse, being an inexperienced horsewoman. But both the gentlemen had mules, and both the gentlemen's mules were the best. Poor Mary colored, and looked at me in despair.

"I think," I said, "the safest plan will be for my sister to try the horses, and see which suits her the best."

Then the different routes to the water-falls were discussed, and the different Douars or Arab villages where it would be best to have a Diffa, or feast, provided,—Mary's judgment being asked in every instance. All this time the Lieutenant had turned over the leaves of a newspaper very meekly, and the Commandant had caressed his tame gazelle. As soon as she could politely free herself, Mary went up to him.

"How pretty, and playful, and fond it is!" she said, stooping down to stroke the little creature. The grave face of the Commandant brightened.

"Yes; it would be very *triste* here without the little thing."

"Do you never go to France, monsieur?"

"I shall perhaps go in two years' time; but you see, mademoiselle, that is a long time to look forward to; and if my mother should not be living, I might as well stay here."

"Do you like fighting the Arabs in the Desert, then, monsieur?"

"Mademoiselle, when one takes up the profession of arms, fighting and exile are *choses entendues*. I often sigh for a settled, domestic life; but I might have been worse off. I might have gone to Mexico, for instance."

The Commandant's manner was so simple, so manly, and so tinged with sadness, that I think any woman would have sympathized with him as much as my little sister Mary did. She, poor child, having lived all her life in a school-room, was quite ready to make a hero of any man that smiled kindly upon her; and here were four heroes, in handsome uniforms, all smiling upon her at once! There was the sweet sense of youth drawing her to the Lieutenant; but I think the Commandant stood next in her favor, and she could not for a moment forget the courteous kindness of the other two.

"It must all be a dream, Tom," she said, as she gave me her good-night kiss; "but, oh! if it is a dream, don't let me wake yet."

We dreamed some wonderful things in the next few days. Dominique made us get up, one morning, very early, and drove us in his little wooden gig to an Arab encampment miles away in the Desert. It was dawn when we started, and large, pale stars were shining in a violet sky; then, like a gorgeous butterfly emerging from a dusky chrysalis, came the Eastern day, and we felt as if living in a world warmed by a hundred suns. The warm, intoxicating light took possession of our senses, and so sweet, so rarefied, so indescribably delicious was the air, that it seemed to give wings to our dull bodies. Every now and then we were overtaken by clouds of locusts, their little wings glistening like diamonds against the soft sky, or flocks of starlings darkened the air, or a serried line of wild geese passed majestically overhead. Then we came to the tents, and at our approach a dozen dogs rushed out to snap and snarl, and a hundred little naked children scampered and scuttled across the way. A stately Bedouin made us welcome, and, while Dominique transacted business with him, his women gathered around us, chattering and grinning like children. Then we were feasted upon cous-cous-sou and figs, and took leave, after many "salamaleks."

Another day we went out hunting gazelles, bivouacking along a riverside, and feasting, Arab fashion, off a sheep roasted whole. Dominique had found a pretty little French girl, daughter of a travelling farrier, to act as Mary's handmaid; and she now felt less isolated among so many men, and less shy, too. The poor child stood a fair chance of being spoiled, what with suddenly finding herself transformed from a school-room Cinderella to a fairy-tale princess, and having four lovers, all heroes, at once. For it was impossible to deny that the Général, the Commandant, the Capitaine, and the Lieutenant all behaved like lovers, presenting her with jackal skins, ostrich plumes and eggs, rare birds, and other treasures of the Sahara. The Général went so far as to give her a little negro boy about ten years old, though this gift we had accepted only temporarily, not quite knowing what to do with him when we left Teschoun.

Christmas-day came at last. Mary had artfully evaded the delicate point about horses by declaring herself afraid of every one's beast but Dominique's; accordingly, mounted on Dominique's ugly hack, she led the way with the Général, her long, bright hair flowing in curls over her shoulders, her cheeks glowing with excitement. The pleasure and picturesqueness of the last few days—for Mary had an artistic perception of beauty—had brought out a new side to her character; and she quite surprised me, from time to time, with her saucy humor and quick repartee.

We made a brilliant cavalcade, what with the uniforms of the officers, and the richly embroidered saddles and bright-red burnouses of our attendant spahis. After riding some miles across a monotonous tract of stony desert, we came to a majestic sierra of crag, down which fell a dozen water-falls, narrow and bright as sword-blades. A thin little stream threaded the ravine, and on its banks grew clumps of the tamarisk, the oleander, and the thuya, making an oasis grateful to the eyes. Here we sat down and ate our Christmas breakfast, with stray thoughts of village bells chiming at home, and school children lustily singing their Christmas hymns.

Our host, the Capitaine, had provided a sumptuous feast of Desert fare,—roast quails and plovers, cous-cous-sou, figs, dates, and bananas, with the addition of champagne; and we were very merry.

"Mademoiselle," said the Capitaine, "think what our next Christmas will be if you are not here. Persuade monsieur, your brother, to purchase some land between Mascara and Teschoun, so that we shall not lose you altogether."

The Général nudged the Commandant.

"You see what our friend the Capitaine is dreaming of! Mon Capitaine, your escadron is sure to be sent into the interior this spring; put all romances out of your head, my dear fellow, and do not entice monsieur into the committal of follies."

"I am not the only one to entertain romances," said the Capitaine, coolly. "You, mon Général, did us all the honor to spend Christmas at Teschoun. We can but attribute such a condescension to the gracious influence of mademoiselle."

"Look well after the Commandant when I am gone, gentlemen," continued the Général, looking round with a smile. "Matters are gone so far already that he loses his temper if a fellow-officer but jests with him. What a terrible slur it would be upon the glorious annals of French-African conquest, if such a brave officer should show himself fonder of stuffing birds for an English demoiselle than running swords through ungrateful Arabs!" and the Général looked round with a very comical expression of mock horror.

"Mademoiselle has indiscriminately accepted our tokens of homage," the Commandant said, maliciously.

"But it yet remains to be seen whose offering has been most acceptable to her," went on the Général, adding, *au grand sérieux*, "we won't resort to duels unless absolutely necessary."

This sort of banter lasted so long that poor Mary's cheeks burned with mixed vanity and mortification, and she made an excuse to leave us.

"And what does our Lieutenant advise monsieur to do?" asked the Général,—"to settle here, or to follow his escadron to the Desert?" Whereupon the poor Lieutenant colored, and said nothing.

What an experience it was, that Christmas-day in the Desert! The noonday sun seemed to dissolve in the warm atmosphere, and, instead of a single orb shining overhead, large and golden, we had melted suns innumerable about us, and almost lost the sense of corporeity in their charmed medium.

When the short bright day waned, and the large stars were coming out one by one, we found ourselves near home; and when the heavens had turned to bluish-black, and the stars to splendid silvery moons, we passed under the gate of Teschoun, and saw our shadows, darker and deeper than real things, fall across the white walls of mosque and fortress. For shadow and substance lost their identity in the Desert and one is always on the point of mistaking the one for the other: if anything, shadow is the more real of the two.

So absorbed was I in the suggestions of this mysterious beauty, that I had forgotten all about my sister's lovers till we were fairly in our little sitting-room. Then Mary began to sigh and blush, and to hint that she thought we had better leave Teschoun very soon.

"You see, Tom, dear," she said, with tears in her eyes, "the Général says he adores me, and the Commandant says he never loved any one in the world until he saw me, and the Capitaine says that if I go away he will blow his brains out, and what am I to do?"

"And the Lieutenant,—what did he say?"

"He says nothing," said Mary, looking down; "and,"—here came a sob,—"and I like him best of all!"

"But, if he does not declare the same liking for you, we must leave him out of the question, and choose between the other three, I suppose."

"He does not speak because he is too modest: I'm sure he likes me," Mary added, still ready to cry.

"His state of feeling does not help us much, unless expressed," I replied. "Meantime, what am I to say to the Général, the Commandant, and the Capitaine, if they ask to marry you?"

The little thing plucked at the folds of her riding-skirt in the greatest perplexity.

"I like the Général and I like the Commandant, and I ought not to dislike the Capitaine; but I cannot marry one without offending the others; and, if I were to marry out here in the Desert, Tom, would you stay, too?"

We had been living in such utter fairy-land lately, that I felt as if it were quite possible for me to marry some brown-skinned, soft-eyed Rebecca, and turn Mahometan. But, in any case, could I desire for my sister a happier fate than to marry one of these brave gentlemen, and live in the sunny South all the rest of her days? She would be rescued from a life of toil and friendlessness, and have another protector besides her Bohemian of a brother.

"My dear child," I said, "it would be impossible for me to say that our lives should be spent together; but you may be quite sure that nothing would utterly divide them. The chief point is, of all your lovers, whom do you love?"

To this question I could elicit no positive reply. Mary, in fact, was half in love with the Général and the Commandant, and wholly in love with the Lieutenant, and was quite incapable of deciding her own fate.

"You must not laugh at me," she said, simply, as we bade each other good-night; "it is so new to me to have lovers, and so delightful, that I wish I could go on forever being happy, and making them happy, without marrying either." Then she blushed and ran off to bed.

The next morning we were taking our early coffee, when we heard the clatter of horses' feet, and, looking out, saw one of the Général's splendid, brown-skinned, red-cloaked spahis dashing into the town at a furious rate. He pulled up at Dominique's door, and, letting his little barb prance and rear at will, looked towards us, showing his white teeth and waving a letter in one hand.

I left my breakfast and ran down to him. We exchanged "salamaleks," and then he put the letter in my hand, adding, in broken French, "Le Général,—envoyer cela,—va faire le guerre,—la-bas." Then he put spurs to his horse's flanks, and dashed away as fast as he had come.

I broke the seal of the Général's letter, which ran as follows:

"Monsieur,—This morning at daybreak I received telegraphic information that a serious rising has taken place among the tribes southward of Fig-gig, and I have resolved to march upon them without delay. Judge, monsieur, how more than sorry I am to be forced to quit the society of your charming sister and yourself without making my adieux; but a soldier's duty forces him from the consummation of his fondest desires, when such a consummation seems close at hand, and I go, if not with joy, at least without soldierly reluctance. I shall never forget, monsieur, this episode, an oasis in the desert of my military life; and, while wishing for mademoiselle and yourself all possible prosperity, I hope you will remember Teschoun and the poor exiled officers there, who will never think of you both without regret.

"I feel it right, under the grave circumstances of the revolt, to advise your speedy return to Mascara, and will order a trusty escort to be in readiness for you when you shall require it.

"Meantime, receive, monsieur, the expression of my utmost esteem.

"De Marion."

We were both of us talking over the astounding contents of the Général's letter, when Napoleon came in, full of news. The insurgents numbered thousands, and there were skirmishing parties close to Teschoun. Teschoun would be most likely besieged, as it had been more than once, etc., etc. As the day wore on, the excitement increased. Little groups of French or Jewish shopkeepers collected together and talked gravely, Arabs walked about in stately fashion, smiling superciliously. In the French camp it was the old story on a lesser scale:

> "And there was mounting in hot haste; the steed,
> The mustering squadron, and the clattering car
> Went pouring forward with impetuous speed."

And so great was the need for hurry that we doubted whether we should see either of our gallant hosts again. Late in the afternoon, however, the Capitaine paid us a formal, sentimental visit, and after him came the Commandant, who stood up before us, square and stiff, and stammered out a word or two with tears in his kind eyes. Mary held out her little hand; but he seemed overcome with shyness or sadness, or both, and rushed away without having taken it.

Last of all, when we had quite given him up, came the poor Lieutenant: he had been busy on a hundred errands for his superior officers, and had only five minutes to spare. We can never do anything with a few last moments, and Mary and the

Lieutenant had not a word to say to each other, though I could see well enough what both would fain have said.

So I quietly left them under the pretext of fetching a cigar, and when I returned, at the close of the fifth minute, all that was necessary had been said. We then embraced each other after the hearty French fashion. Mary and the Lieutenant exchanged rings, and he went off to fight the disaffected Arabs as happy as a king!

It was a fine sight to see the troops march out of Teschoun. Color is really color in the South, and the lines of blue zouaves and crimson spahis against the mellow afternoon sky were vivid and picturesque beyond description.

On they went, arms flashing, drums beating, colors flying, till the last column had turned the hill, and then evening came on all at once, and we felt a dreary sense of disenchantment creeping over us. It was as if we had been dreaming during the last few weeks, and now we were waked, indeed! Dominique recalled us to ourselves with a cynical smile.

"Bah!" he cries, "it's all play; let 'em pretend to put down insurrection as often as they please. It is good for trade and promotion, and the Arabs know how to defend themselves."

But events falsified this sarcasm of Monsieur Dominique's, for the insurrection proved serious, and it was months before we heard of our Lieutenant. When we did hear, the news was good; and the news of him and of his English wife—dowered by our Vittoria Colonna—has been good ever since.

The End

www.ingramcontent.com/pod-product-compliance
Lightning Source LLC
Chambersburg PA
CBHW070648290526
45790CB00001B/222